THE GROUNDBREAKING WORK ON KARATE

KARATE

The Art of "Empty Hand" Fighting

Hidetaka Nishiyama
and Richard C. Brown

With a new foreword
by **Ray Dalke**, 8th
Highest-ranking American
Shotokan Karate

TUTTLE Publishing
Tokyo | Rutland, Vermont | Singapore

Contents

PART 1:
Introduction

PART 2:
Basic Techniques and Their Practice

PART 3:
Karate as Self-Defense

Foreword

Hidetaka Nishiyama's groundbreaking work *Karate: The Art of "Empty Hand" Fighting* was the only technical study of karate available in English when it was originally published in 1957. Today, while there are many karate books to choose from, Nishiyama's work remains the foundation for all others with its clear comprehension of the art.

During my thirty years as director of the martial arts program at the University of California, Riverside, this book was the primary textbook for all karate classes. Thousands of students relied on it as their "go-to" text for deeper study of the art. Nishiyama believed that it was important for students to follow a training schedule, allowing them to develop along a smooth, step-by-step learning curve. A schedule reinforces important points, including mistakes to avoid (as this will lead the practitioner to perfection of technique), an emphasis on combinations of techniques (in order to achieve physical and mental balance) and small nuances in explanations (these will lead the reader to maximize development of technique).

As I reread the book in preparation to write this foreword, I was again struck by the depth of Nishiyama's knowledge and the conciseness and structured style he used to present his lessons. Students of karate will find this book to be an essential source for truly understanding the art's principles, dynamics, and techniques.

Nishiyama does not differentiate among the different styles of karate, nor does he advocate for any one. Instead he relates to them all in regard to their individual techniques. His analysis of the art from the standpoint of physics, physiology, philosophy, and body dynamics applies to all styles. Understanding these principles will result in maximizing the practitioner's technique and, with training, exceeding those maximums.

The theories in this book were developed when Nishiyama was chief instructor of the Japan Karate Association (JKA) Instructor Training Program; his research was utilized in the classes he taught to his selected protégés—Hirokazu Kanazawa, Hiroshi Shirai, and Keinosuke Enoeda, among others. His knowledge and understanding of the science related to karate was truly ahead of its time. A practitioner who studies this book and trains in karate can be assured,

"You may not be a world champion, but you will be better than you are today."

Nishiyama was a man with a dream to spread karate throughout the world. He aimed to do this by sending his JKA instructors to teach in various countries. This book represents the start of that venture. His plan continued when he arrived in Los Angeles in 1961.

I met Sensei Nishiyama upon his arrival in Southern California and remained with him until his passing in 2008. He arrived as a thirty-one-year-old full of life and ambition. He was a serious, private man who established himself as the leader among his peers—of whom there were few. My introduction to the man, the teacher, the instructor who would dedicate his entire life to the development of the art of karate began when he opened his dojo in downtown Los Angeles.

The dojo was a 5,000-square-foot building—clean, simple, and unadorned except for American and Japanese flags placed on the main wall with a picture of Gichin Funakoshi, the "Father of Modern Karate," between them. There were polished hardwood floors and mirrors on one wall. Upon entering, there was a smell of sweat and Salonpas but there was also a feeling of excitement that permeated throughout the building. Always early to the dojo and always the last to leave, Sensei was disciplined, as his work ethic proved.

English wasn't his native tongue, and he ended up speaking a combination of broken English and Japanese. These didn't mix well. We all had to pay attention and learn by watching his physical demonstration of technique while he attempted to explain important points. For us students this was very challenging, but we were fortunate to be able to refer to his book.

He inspired tremendous energy and enthusiasm in his students, challenging each one of us to think and perform. His command of "one more time!" echoed throughout his classes. His looks of approval were few and far between, but they were what we worked for—those special positive nods of his head.

He paced around his classes like an animal trainer, searching for mistakes in technique, correcting then reminding us what not to do. His command was never challenged, as his classes were strict. There were no opportunities for us to ask questions. As large as the classes were, his demand for technical perfection left each of us with a sense that the class was designed specifically for us individually. The classes always included a review of our previous work, then on to a new technique. Classes were two to three hours long with no break, leaving us tired and sweaty yet invigorated and motivated to do more.

Sensei was a consummate teacher—a teacher's teacher—never violating the student-instructor relationship, never showing weakness or pain, never revealing his personal life. For forty-seven years I was a student, never a friend. Yet he was the godfather to my son, Christopher Hideo.

In 1961, when I began training, it was explained to me that Sensei wanted to organize a group of students to train in the very serious karate he had trained his students in in Japan. These students must not care about breaking bones or brutal training methods. He wanted total commitment and dedication to the art. He really wanted a team to match his students in Japan—Shirai, Enoeda, and Kanazawa.

America was a little more than a decade past two wars—World War II and Korea—in the middle of a Cold War and with the Cuban Missile Crisis and Vietnam on the horizon. I was ready for blood-and-guts training, as were most of the students in the dojo at that time. The ones who weren't, as a result of the grueling methods (especially sparring), left. I loved it. We loved it. Sensei loved it.

What Sensei enjoyed most was having his team square up against Japanese instructors or guests that were invited to visit. His team would challenge the visitors in technique and, in many cases, better them. He would show a sly smile as he appreciated the results of his instruction.

The technical knowledge he gave to his students, through training and teaching, created great American champions like James Yabe, Frank Smith, Greer Golden, Rei Fujikawa, and James Field. All were multiple winners in *kata* and *kumite*, and I was honored to be a part of that team, that group, that era. These were the great years at the dawn of worldwide karate, and during that entire time this book was at the center of it all.

There is no magic or mysticism to the art of karate (or this book) and there was no magic or mysticism to Sensei Nishiyama. His guiding message was to maximize the potential of the human body and to succeed through rigorous training. In his many years of teaching thousands of classes he never wavered from that philosophy. I have trained with other instructors, but never at the level of comprehensive instruction offered by Sensei Nishiyama. Writing this foreword allows me the opportunity to say, "Thank you, Sensei." Thank you for organizing my thinking and putting me on a path to professional and personal success—for giving me a life of purpose.

As an observer for nearly five decades of this man with a dream, I ask, "Did he realize it?"—Oh, yes! In a very big way. Never sacrificing his principles, never wavering from his technique and never changing his philosophy for realizing his dream of the advancement of karate, he touched the world. *Karate: The Art of "Empty Hand" Fighting* represents the beginning of that dream, yet it is more than that. It is the foundation for all karate—throughout the world it is truly the "Bible of Karate."

Ray Dalke

Foreword to the First Edition

It became apparent a few years ago that the growing interest which many foreigners, both in Japan and abroad, had begun to show in karate was more than a superficial attraction to the exotic. Since there was virtually nothing available in English, we realized that there was now a real need for a thorough introduction to karate in all its aspects, with specific instruction in learning and practicing individual techniques.

Because of the almost uncanny striking power which a trained karate practitioner can demonstrate, public exhibitions have tended to emphasize dramatic acts of splitting boards and cracking roof tiles with the bare hands, leaving the impression with many that this was the be-all and end-all of karate. Likewise, the ability to perform such seemingly unbelievable feats has made karate subject to exploitation by those who would claim the possession of mystical or supernatural powers.

In addition to dispelling some of these misconceptions, what we have tried to present is a sober and rational introduction to karate in its three main aspects—as a healthful physical art, as an effective form of self-defense, and as an exciting sport. If this book succeeds in teaching the reader the main elements of true karate and encourages him to learn and practice it, we shall feel that our efforts have been amply rewarded.

We wish to acknowledge our thanks and indebtedness to Teruyuki Okazaki and Hirokazu Kanazawa, instructors of the Japan Karate Association, who so willingly lent us their time and skill in posing for many of the photographs, and to Seizo Ishiba, of the Gineisha Company, who undertook the arduous task of taking most of the photographs, many of which had to be taken more than once because they involved catching a technique in actual full-speed performance.

Hidetaka Nishiyama
Instructor, Japan Karate Association

Richard C. Brown
Member, Japan Karate Association

Disclaimer

Please note that the publisher and author(s) of this instructional book are **NOT RESPONSIBLE** for any injury that may result from practicing the techniques and/or following the instructions given. Martial arts training can be dangerous—both to you and to others—if not practiced safely. You should always consult with a trained martial arts teacher before practicing any of these techniques, and ask them to guide you in the proper techniques to be used. Since the physical activities described herein may be too strenuous in nature for some readers, it is essential that a physician be consulted prior to training.

PART 1
Introduction

1

What Is Karate?

The literal meaning of the two Japanese characters which make up the word *karate* is "empty hands." This, of course, refers simply to the fact that karate originated as a system of self-defense which relied on the effective use of the unarmed body of its practitioner. This system consisted of techniques of blocking or thwarting an attack and counterattacking the opponent by punching, striking, or kicking. The modern art of karate was developed out of a more thorough organization and rationalization of these techniques. And the three branches of present-day karate—as a physical art, as a sport, and as self-defense—are all based on the use of these same fundamental techniques.

Karate as a means of self-defense has the oldest history, going back hundreds of years, but it is only in recent years that the techniques which have been handed down were scientifically studied and principles evolved for making the most effective use of the various movements of the body. Training based on these principles and knowledge of the working of the muscles and joints and the vital relation between movement and balance enable the modern student of karate to be prepared, both physically and psychologically, to defend himself successfully against any would-be assailant.

As a physical art, karate is almost without equal. Since it is highly dynamic and makes balanced use of a large number of body muscles, it provides excellent all-around exercise, and develops coordination and agility. Many girls and women in Japan have taken up karate, since in addition to its usefulness as self-defense, it is especially good for the figure. It is widely practiced by both children and older people as a means of keeping in top physical shape, and many schools are promoting it as a physical art among their students.

As a sport, karate has a relatively short history. However, contest rules have been devised, and it is now possible to hold actual matches, as in other competitive sports. Because of the speed and variety of its techniques and the split-second timing it calls for, many athletic-minded people have come to show an interest in competitive karate, and there is every indication that it will continue to grow in popularity.

Western (i.e., non-Japanese) students of karate may be interested to know that the Japan Karate Association emphasizes its character-building aspects, in which respect for one's opponent, or sportsmanship, is the cardinal principle. The maxims which they teach to their students can be summarized in the following five words:

- Character
- Sincerity
- Effort
- Etiquette
- Self-control

Standing bow performed before and after sparring practice

Class bow to instructors peformed before and after training sessions

2
A Short History

Although the basic forms of individual self-defense are probably as old as the human race, the art of karate as it is practiced today can be traced directly to the Okinawan technique called *Okinawa-te* (Okinawa hands) in Japanese. This system of self-defense in turn is a descendant of the ancient Chinese art of *ch'uan-fa or kempō* (fist way).

There is a famous Chinese legend regarding the origin of *kempō*: The renowned Indian Buddhist monk Daruma Taishi journeyed overland from India to China to instruct the Liang-dynasty monarch on the tenets of Buddhism. To make that long, dangerous journey alone—along a route that is almost impassable even today—is no mean feat, and testifies to Daruma's powers of physical and mental endurance. He remained in China at a monastery called Shaolin-szu and taught Buddhism to the Chinese monks there. Tradition relates how the severe discipline Daruma imposed and the pace he set caused all of the student-monks to pass out, one by one, from sheer physical exhaustion. At the next assembly he explained to them that, although the aim of Buddhism is the salvation of the soul, the body and soul are inseparable, and in their weakened physical state they could never perform the ascetic practices necessary for the

This drawing is a copy of an ancient Chinese painting depicting a karate-like form of unarmed self-defense.

attainment of true enlightenment. To remedy the situation he began to teach them a system of physical and mental discipline embodied in the I-Chin sutra. As time went on, the monks at Shaolin-szu won the reputation of being the most formidable fighters in China. In later years, the art which they practiced came to be called Shaolin-szu "fist way" and formed the basis for present-day China's national sport.

Okinawa is the main island of the Ryukyu Island chain, which is scattered like stepping-stones southwest from southern Kyushu to Taiwan in the East China Sea. From ancient times, Okinawa was in contact with both China and Japan, and probably *kempō* was imported along with many other elements of Chinese culture. Around 1600 China replaced its civil envoys to Okinawa with military men, among whom were many noted for their prowess in Chinese *kempō*. The Okinawans took a keen interest in it and combined it with a native form of hand-to-hand fighting to produce Okinawa-te.

Little is known about the historical development of karate in Okinawa, but there is an interesting story told about it. About five hundred years ago, the famous King Hashi of the Okinawan Sho dynasty succeeded in uniting the Ryukyu Islands into one kingdom. To ensure rule by law and to discourage any potential military rivals, he seized all weapons in the kingdom and made the possession of weapons a crime against the state. About two hundred years later, Okinawa became part of the domain of the Satsuma clan of Kyushu, and for a second time all weapons were seized and banned. As a direct result of these successive bans against weapons, it is said that the art of empty-handed self-defense called Okinawa-te underwent tremendous development.

The man most responsible for the systemization of karate as we know it today was Gichin Funakoshi. He was born in Shuri, Okinawa, in 1869, and when only a boy of eleven began to study karate under the two top masters of the art at that time. In time he became a karate expert in his own right. He is credited with being the first man to introduce karate to Japan proper, when he gave exhibitions in 1917 and again in 1922 at physical education expositions sponsored by the Ministry of Education. The art soon caught on in Japan, and Funakoshi traveled throughout the country giving lectures and demonstrations. The main universities invited him to help them set up karate teams,

Gichin Funakoshi: founder of present-day karate

and hundreds of people studied the art under his guidance.

As the study of karate in Japan became increasingly popular, many other experts from Okinawa and China came to give instruction. At the same time, the ancient native Japanese hand-to-hand fighting techniques of *jūjutsu* as well as *kendō* (sword fighting) were being widely practiced, and modern sports imported from the West were rapidly becoming popular. Karate soon took over many elements from both of these, and the basis was laid for the modern Japanese-style karate described in this book.

In 1948 the Japan Karate Association was organized, with Funakoshi as the chief instructor. Because this organization made it possible for the leading karate men to pool their knowledge and ability, from that time onward progress was rapid, leading to the development of the three aspects of present-day karate; i.e., as self-defense, as a physical art, and as a sport.

In April 1957, Funakoshi, the father of modern karate, passed away at the advanced age of eighty-eight. But tens of thousands of karate practitioners who learned under him remain, insuring that the art which he taught will not die with him. On the contrary, people in many foreign countries have shown an interest in learning karate, and it is rapidly moving toward becoming a world art.

3
Essential Principles

The remarkable strength manifested by many individual karate techniques, both offensive and defensive, is not the mysterious, esoteric thing many observers, as well as certain proponents of the art itself, would have you believe. On the contrary, it is the inevitable result of the effective application of certain well-known scientific principles to the movements of the body. Likewise, knowledge of psychological principles, along with constant practice, enable the karate man to find openings and execute the proper techniques at the proper times, no matter how minute the movements of his opponent. At an advanced level, it is even possible for a karate expert to sense the movements of his opponent before they take place.

Before learning the various individual techniques, it is necessary to have a clear understanding of the physical, psychological, and combined physical-psychological principles which underlie them all. Of course, it is difficult to interpret complicated physical or psychological processes in terms of a few simple principles. Discussed below are the most important ones.

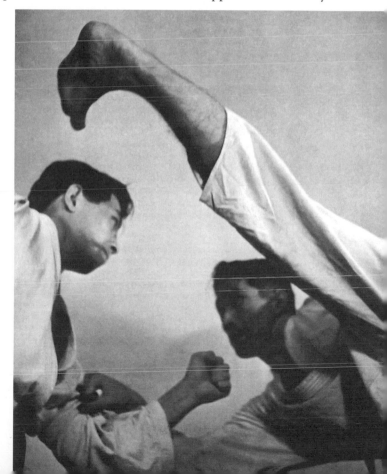

Physical Principles

Maximum strength

Any movement of the body depends on muscular expansion and contraction. There are many factors involved in exerting maximum force through control of these expansions and contractions, and only the most basic are listed here.

- Force is directly proportionate to the degree of muscular expansion and contraction. This is the principle behind, for example, the coil spring—the more the coil is pressed down, the greater the force it exerts when released. Many parts of the human body operate the same way.

- The striking power of a force is inversely proportionate to the time required for its application. This means that in karate it is not the muscular strength used to lift a heavy object that is required, but the strength manifested in terms of speed of muscular expansion and contraction. In other words, force is accumulated in the form of speed, and at the end of the movement, speed is converted into striking force. In scientific language, force equals mass times the square of the velocity.

Concentration of strength

To perform any kind of heavy physical work, concentration of strength is necessary. Even a great amount of strength will accomplish little if it is dispersed. By the same token, a small amount of strength, properly concentrated, can be quite powerful. It is no exaggeration to say that the practice of most karate techniques is the practice of concentration of strength at the proper time and at the proper place. The following principles are basic:

- Other things being equal, the shorter the time a striking force is applied, the more effective it is. This element of concentration in terms of time is very important in karate, for it enables one to move immediately into the next technique.

- The greater the number of muscles brought into play in performing a given movement, the greater the concentration of strength. The force which can be exerted by the hands or feet acting alone is relatively small; therefore, the muscular power of the whole body should be exerted in such a way that this strength is concentrated at the point of impact.

- Maximum concentration of body strength depends on effective utilization of the resultant forces produced by exertion of the various muscles. When the muscles are properly coordinated, the resultant force is greater; when they act in opposite directions, it is lessened.

- Concentration of strength depends not on simultaneous exertion of all the body muscles, but on their exertion in the proper order. The muscles of the abdominal and pelvic region are powerful but slow, whereas those of the extremities are fast but weak. In order to concentrate the force of both sets of muscles, those of the abdomen and hips must be brought into play first, and this force transferred to the point of impact, either in the hands or feet. This accounts for the common saying in karate that one should move the hips first and the hands and feet last.

Utilizing reaction force
This refers to the well-known principle of physics that to every action there is an opposite and equal reaction. This principle finds wide use in karate; for example, in punching out with one hand, the other hand is simultaneously withdrawn to the hip, adding reaction force to the punching hand. Running or jumping is made possible by pressing downward with the opposite foot. This is an important feature in karate where, for example, in punching, the rear leg is pressed hard against the floor, and the resulting reaction force is passed through the body and arm to the striking hand, adding force to the punch. In even more complex fashion, when the hand actually strikes the target, the shock of the blow is passed through the body to the legs and floor and then is reversed back to the punching hand, adding further force to the blow.

Use of breath control
It is well-known that exhaling aids in contracting the muscles, while inhaling tends to relax the muscles. This finds direct application in karate, where the breath is sharply exhaled during the execution of techniques and inhaled after their completion.

Psychological Principles

Since karate involves direct contact between two or more human beings, psychological factors play an important role. In many cases the psychologically stronger party wins even when he is outmatched physically. Although this psychological conditioning comes about naturally—until it is almost second nature—in the course of karate training, the examples given below, which embody ancient concepts handed down from the past, offer valuable avenues of approach.

Mizu no kokoro (mind like water)
This term, along with the one in the following section, was emphasized in the teachings of the ancient karate masters. Both refer to the mental attitude

required while facing an actual opponent. *Mizu no kokoro* refers to the need to make the mind calm, like the surface of undisturbed water. To carry the symbolism further, smooth water reflects accurately the image of all objects within its range, and if the mind is kept in this state, apprehension of the opponent's movements, both psychological and physical, will be both immediate and accurate, and one's responses, both defensive and offensive, will be appropriate and adequate. On the other hand, if the surface of the water is disturbed, the images it reflects will be distorted; or by analogy, if the mind is preoccupied with thoughts of attack or defense, it will not apprehend the opponent's intentions, creating an opportunity for the opponent to attack.

Tsuki no kokoro (mind like the moon)

This concept refers to the need to be constantly aware of the totality of the opponent and his movements, just as moonlight shines equally on everything within its range. With the thorough development of this attitude, the consciousness will be immediately aware of any opening in the opponent's defenses. Clouds blocking the light of the moon are likened to nervousness or distractions which interfere with correct apprehension of the opponent's movements and make it impossible to find an opening and to apply the proper techniques.

Unity of mind and will

To use a modern analogy, if the mind is compared to the speaker of a telephone, the will is like the electric current. No matter how sensitive the speaker is, if there is no electric current, no communication takes place. Similarly, even if you correctly apprehend the movements of your opponent and are conscious of an opening, if the will to act on this knowledge is lacking, no effective technique will be forthcoming. The mind may find an opening, but the will must be activated in order to execute the technique called for.

Combined Physical-Psychological Principles

Focus (*kime*)

Briefly, "focus" in karate refers to the concentration of all the energy of the body in an instant on a specific target. This involves not only concentration of physical strength but also the type of mental concentration described above. There is no such thing as a focus lasting for any measurable length of time. Since successful karate depends entirely on effective concentration of body strength, focus is extremely important, and without it karate would become nothing more than a form of dancing. This principle will appear frequently in the following pages, so a clear understanding of it at this point is desirable. To further analyze the concept of focus, take the technique of punching as an example. In reverse punching, the fist is thrust straight out from the body and simultaneously the hips are twisted in the direction of the punch so as to transmit the strength of the hips and trunk to the face of the fist, augmenting its speed and power. Of course, speed and power must be carefully balanced; sacrificing speed by exerting too much power into the arm or body must be avoided. Also, the breath control principle explained above plays an important part in focusing; i.e., the breath should be sharply exhaled at the moment of impact. And, of course, there must be an accompanying mental attitude reflecting this total concentration of the body's strength. As the fist nears the target its speed is increased to its maximum point, and at the moment of impact the muscles of the entire body are tensed. The effect of this is that speed is transformed into power, and the strength of the entire body is concentrated for an instant at the fist. This, in essence, is what "focus" in karate means.

It should not be forgotten that this maximum exertion of energy is instantaneous and in the next instant is withdrawn in preparation for the next movement; i.e., the muscles are relaxed, the breath inhaled, and a position appropriate for the next technique assumed. A karate technique which is not focused is ineffective and so much wasted effort.

Responding (*hen-ō*)

This karate concept refers to the correct apprehension of the opponent's movements and the conscious adoption of the proper techniques in accordance with them. Both parts of this process are performed as a single momentary act and appear to an onlooker almost as a reflex action. It is this character of karate that creates self-confidence in its practitioner; i.e., he knows that his mind-directed reflexes don't have to "think" what to do.

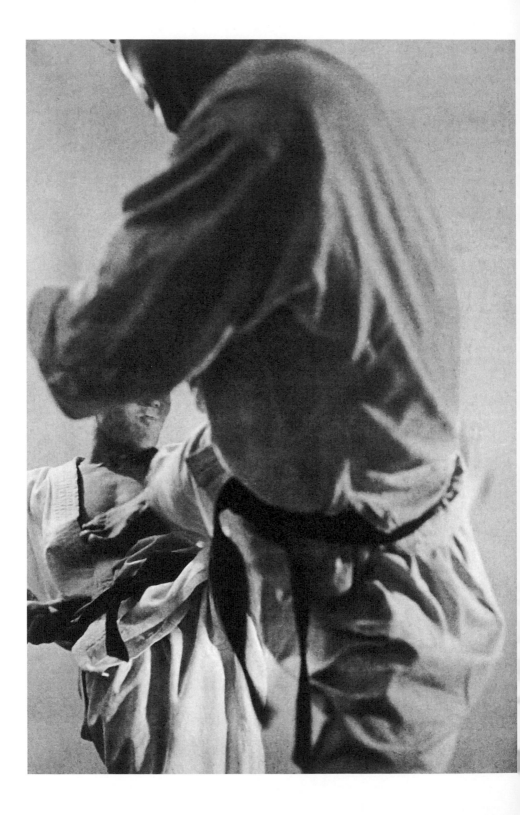

4

Organization of Karate Techniques

Karate techniques, like the techniques of any other highly developed sport or physical art, have been organized over the years into a distinct system. Before giving instruction in the individual techniques, it may be worthwhile to outline the essentials of this system.

Overall Organization of Karate Techniques

As shown in the following chart, karate techniques can be broken down into two major categories: blocking the opponent's attack and counterattacking. In addition, throwing and joint-twisting techniques are used in certain circumstances.

The major categories of blocking, counterattacking, throwing, and joint-twisting techniques are in turn based on the use of hand techniques, foot

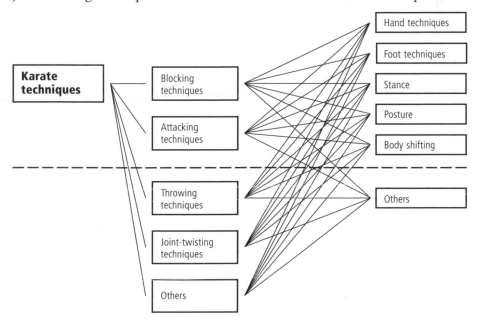

techniques, stance, posture, and body shifting. Since karate is an art based on the maximum use of all parts of the body, various special techniques are occasionally resorted to, such as using parts of the head or striking with the body.

Organization of Hand Techniques

Broadly speaking, hand techniques can be separated into punching (*tsuki-waza*), striking (*uchi-waza*), and hooking (*kake-waza*). As shown on the right side of the following chart, in actual practice, by using particular parts of the hand in various ways, these techniques are broken down into more specific hand techniques.

For example, by punching directly ahead with the front of the fist, the straight punch (*choku-zuki*) is performed. By punching in a semicircular motion, it becomes the roundhouse punch (*mawashi-zuki*). The same part of the

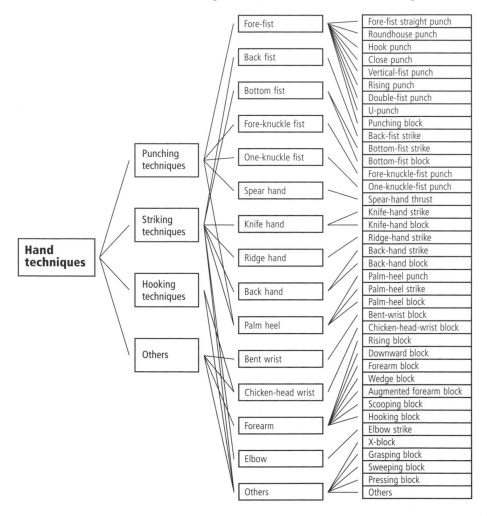

hand used in punching may also be used to perform various kinds of punching blocks (*tsuki-uke*). Similarly, striking with the hand as with a knife is called the knife-hand strike (*shutō-uchi*). Using the same part of the hand for blocking produces the knife-hand block (*shutō-uke*).

Organization of Foot Techniques

Foot techniques may be broadly divided into kicking (*keri-waza*), stamping (*fumi-waza*), and miscellaneous. By using specific parts of the foot in various ways, specific foot techniques may be performed.

For example, by kicking with the ball of the foot, the front snap kick (*mae-geri-keage*), the front thrust kick (*mae-geri-kekomi*), the roundhouse kick (*mawashi-geri*), and the flying front kick (*mae-tobi-geri*) may be performed. Again, striking with the knee becomes the knee kick (*hittsui-geri*), and so on.

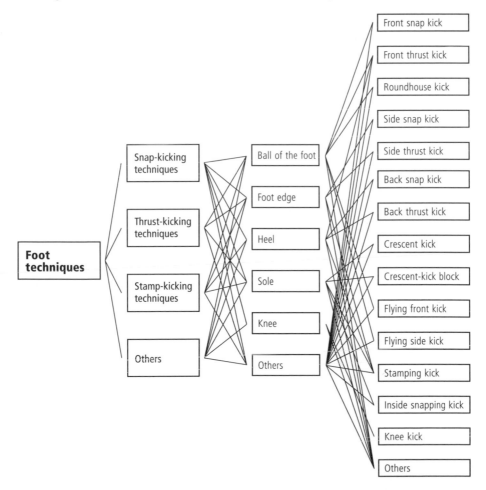

Organization of Stances

Stances may be broken into natural stances, in which the muscles are relaxed, stances where the legs are put under tension by forcing the knees outward, and those where the legs are put under tension by forcing the knees inward. As these are adapted to specific purposes, they become specific kinds of stances.

The natural stances are preparatory to moving into a specific technique, while those in which the legs are kept under tension help in maintaining balance and add strength to both blocking and counterattacking techniques.

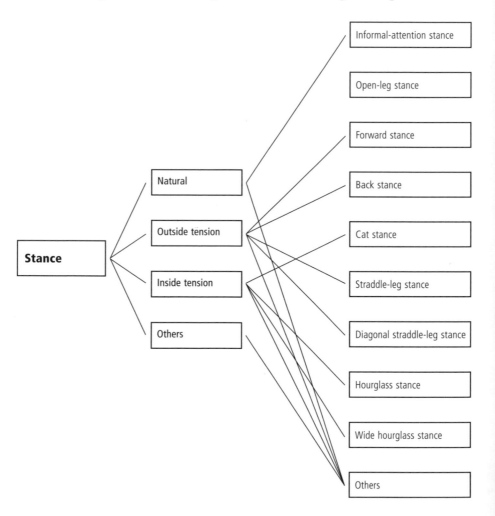

Organization of Posture

There are postures in which the upper part of the body is vertical to the ground and those where it is not vertical. Each of these is broken down into postures in which one directly faces the opponent, faces him at an oblique angle, or faces him at right angles.

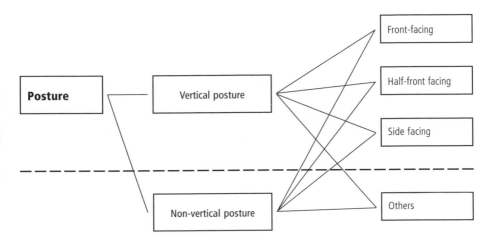

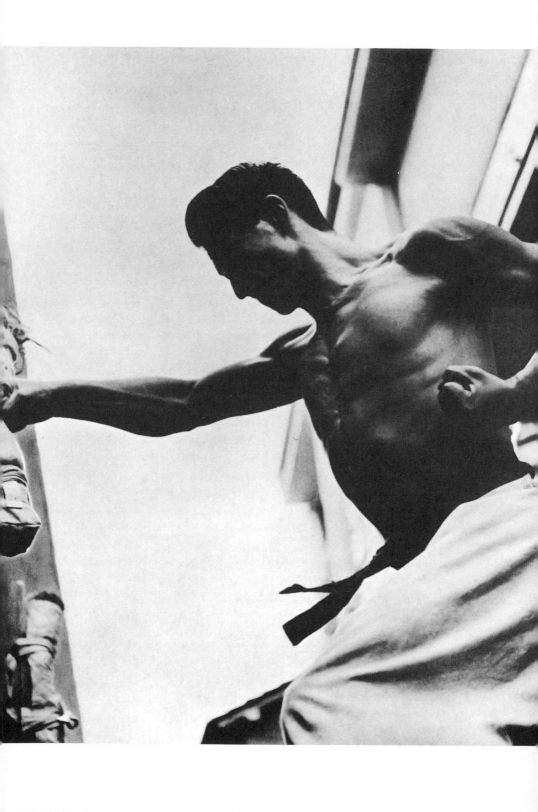

5
Training Methods

The succeeding chapters present the main techniques of karate in systematic form. However, this order does not indicate the proper sequence of learning or the various types of training schedules. Karate training consists of three main aspects: individual training in basic techniques, applied training with an opponent, and auxiliary exercises to increase skills required to perform the various techniques.

The common factor underlying all karate techniques is the concrete application of the laws of physics, anatomy, and psychology in such a way that maximum power can be attained. It is this constant search for ways to apply the laws of science to movements of the body that distinguishes karate from other sports, and the effectiveness of karate techniques themselves is derived from this scientific orientation.

No doubt the average student beginning to study karate finds the basic practice rather dull and would like to go on immediately to the more exciting practical application. But unless he builds a firm foundation in the basic techniques, his progress will eventually be hampered and his lack of skill in the fundamentals will prove to be a bitter handicap.

Karate techniques can be performed both singly and in combination, and it has been proved that the most effective and well-rounded practice session includes both types. Here is an outline example of a typical practice schedule:

1. Basic practice
   a. Punching
   b. Striking
   c. Blocking
   d. Kicking

2. Formal exercise

3. Sparring
   a. Basic sparring
   b. Semi-free sparring
   c. Freestyle sparring

The four most basic components of karate are given under number 1 above. These can be mastered only through constant practice of each one individually.

The formal exercise (2) is composed of all four techniques in combination, plus such body shifting and changes in stance as are required for their smooth performance. These formal exercises give valuable training in mastering the various techniques in combination.

Sparring (3) is a practice method in the form of simulated fighting which gives concrete training in choosing and executing the proper techniques. Especially, it gives training in those techniques which cannot be performed by one person alone; e.g., distancing (see page 173) and responding.

Basic sparring (3a) consists of practice with an opponent in which the mode of attack is prearranged. In freestyle sparring (3c) neither the attack nor the defense is prearranged, and contestants are allowed to punch, strike, block, and kick in the manner of their choosing—taking care, of course, to pull their punches and kicks just short of contact. It is the performance of this freestyle sparring that constitutes competitive karate, and for practice in the combined use of a large number of techniques, it is unsurpassed. Needless to say, freestyle sparring is advanced karate and can be engaged in only after thorough grounding in all the fundamentals. Semi-free sparring is an important intermediate step between basic and freestyle sparring.

The sample training schedule given above is only a basic outline; in actual fact there are many methods of training, which vary according to the aim of the student (as a physical art, for self-defense, or as a sport), his age, strength, level of ability, etc. That is to say, freestyle sparring is emphasized by the younger enthusiasts who enjoy and desire skill in competition. Women are more likely to take up karate both for improving their figures and for self-defense. For children and older people, the emphasis is on the virtues of karate as physical exercise. In all cases, however, the level of skill of the practitioners affects the type of training; beginners must emphasize practice of basic techniques until they have mastered them, whereas experts will devote most of their time to sparring practice.

The following are examples of different types of training schedules:

I. Karate gym for the general public (classes include students, office workers, boys, older men, women, etc., whose aims may include all three aspects of karate; practice is held one hour a day, six days a week)

1. Beginners' training program (four weeks)
   First week
      Basic practice
         a. Stances—natural stances, forward stance
         b. Blocking—downward block

    c. Punching—straight punch, reverse punch
    d. Kicking—front kick

Second week
  Basic practice
    a. Review of first week's material
    b. Blocking—forearm block, rising block

Third week
  Basic practice
    a. Review of first two weeks' material
    b. Stance—straddle-leg stance
    c. Punching—lunge punch
    d. Striking—back-fist strike
    e. Kicking—side kick
  Basic sparring

Fourth week
  Basic practice
    a. Review of first three weeks' material
    b. Stance—back stance
  Formal exercise
  Basic sparring

2. Secondary training program (in this case specific kinds of practice are emphasized on certain days of the week)
  Monday (emphasis on blocking)
    Basic practice—20 minutes
    Sparring
      a. Basic—10 minutes
      b. Freestyle—10 minutes
    Formal exercises—10 minutes
  Tuesday (emphasis on punching)
    Basic practice—20 minutes
    Sparring
      a. Basic—10 minutes
      b. Freestyle—10 minutes
    Formal exercises—30 minutes
  Wednesday (emphasis on stances)
    Basic practice—20 minutes
    Basic sparring—10 minutes
    Formal exercises—30 minutes
  Thursday (emphasis on kicking)
    Basic practice—20 minutes

Sparring
   a. Basic—10 minutes
   b. Freestyle—10 minutes
Friday (emphasis on sparring)
   Basic practice—20 minutes
   Sparring
      a. Basic—10 minutes
      b. Freestyle—20 minutes
   Formal exercises—10 minutes
Saturday (emphasis on formal exercises)
   Basic practice—10 minutes
   Basic sparring—10 minutes
   Formal exercises—30 minutes

II. University karate team (in comparison with the foregoing gym, the practice here is very rigorous, with special emphasis on freestyle sparring, because the competitive aspect is the major aim of the students; beginners must undergo intensive training in the basic techniques)

1. Beginners' course (practice is held two hours a day, six days a week, for sixteen weeks)
   First week
      Basic practice
         a. Stances—natural stance, forward stance
         b. Punching—straight punch, reverse punch
         c. Kicking—front kick
         d. Blocking—downward block
   Second week
      Basic practice—1½ hours
         a. Review of 1st week's material
         b. Stances—straddle-leg stance
         c. Punching—lunge punch
         d. Kicking—side kick
         e. Blocking—rising block, forearm block
      Basic sparring—30 minutes
   Third week
      Basic practice—1 hour
         a. Review
         b. Stances—back stance, cat stance
         c. Striking techniques—elbow strike, knife-hand strike
         d. Kicking—roundhouse kick
         e. Blocking—knife-hand block
      Basic sparring—1 hour

Fourth week
  Basic practice—1 hour
    a. Review
    b. Kicking—back kick
  Formal exercises—30 minutes
  Basic sparring—30 minutes
Fifth to sixteenth week
  Basic practice—40 minutes
    a. Fore-fist straight punch
    b. Reverse punch
    c. Lunge punch
    d. Rising block
    e. Forearm block
    f. Knife-hand block
    g. Forward kick
    h. Side snap kick
    i. Side thrust kick
    j. Roundhouse kick
  Formal exercises—40 minutes
  Basic sparring—40 minutes

2. Advanced class (practice is held 2½ hours a day, six days a week; emphasis is placed on sparring)
  Monday (emphasis on fundamentals)
    Basic practice—30 minutes
      a. Punching
      b. Striking
      c. Blocking
      d. Kicking
    Combination of punching, striking, blocking, and kicking techniques—20 minutes
    Body shifting—20 minutes
    Formal exercises—30 minutes
    Basic sparring—20 minutes
  Tuesday and Friday (emphasis on development of sparring techniques)
    Basic practice—20 minutes
    Combining techniques-20 minutes
    Body shifting—20 minutes
    Sparring research—30 minutes
    Basic sparring—10 minutes
    Semi-free sparring—10 minutes
    Formal exercises—10 minutes

Wednesday, Thursday, and Saturday (emphasis on sparring)
  Basic practice—10 minutes
  Combining techniques—20 minutes
  Semi-free sparring—10 minutes
  Freestyle sparring—40 minutes
  Body shifting—15 minutes
  Formal exercises—15 minutes

Experience has shown that, in general, the body can be kept in the best condition by varying the intensity of the training as follows:
  Sunday—holiday
  Monday—rigorous training
  Tuesday—light training
  Wednesday—normal training
  Thursday—normal training
  Friday—light training
  Saturday—rigorous training

III. Karate team for people with limited time at their disposal (the training course is eight weeks, two hours a day, three days a week; in order to advance as far as possible within this limited period, the first part is devoted to mastering the basic techniques, the latter part to applied techniques; special emphasis is placed on acquiring skill in self-defense)

First week
  Monday—introduction
  Wednesday
    Open-leg stance
    Fore-fist straight punch
    Forward stance
    Front kick
    Reverse punch
  Friday
    Review
    Downward block
    Rising block
Second week
  Monday
    Review
    Straddle-leg stance
    Lunge punch
    Elbow strike

Side thrust kick
Basic sparring
Wednesday
Review
Back stance
Knife-hand block
Side snap kick
Basic sparring
Friday
Review
Roundhouse kick
Forearm block
Basic sparring
Third week
Monday
Review
Body shifting
Basic sparring
Wednesday
Review
Back-fist strike
Spear-hand straight thrust
knife-hand strike
Basic sparring
Friday
Review
Hook punch
Flying kicks
Basic sparring
Fourth week
Monday
Review
Formal exercise
Basic sparring
Wednesday
Review of material learned so far
Friday
Examination
Critique

Fifth week
  Monday
    Review
    Defense against holding
    Basic sparring
  Wednesday
    Review
    Defense against wrestling-style holds
    Defense against holding by two opponents
    Basic sparring
  Friday
    Review of fundamentals
    Review of defense against holding
    Basic sparring
Sixth week
  Monday
    Review of fundamentals
    Freestyle sparring
    Basic sparring
  Wednesday
    Review of fundamentals
    Defense against boxing-style attacks
    Freestyle sparring
    Basic sparring
  Friday
    Review of fundamentals
    Review of defense against boxing-style attacks
    Freestyle sparring
    Basic sparring
Seventh week
  Monday
    Review of fundamentals
    Defense against knife attack
    Basic sparring
  Wednesday
    Review of fundamentals
    Defense against attack by club
    Basic sparring
Eighth week
  Monday

Review of fundamentals
Defense against pistol threat
Freestyle sparring
Basic sparring
Wednesday
Review of all material learned to date
Friday
Examination
Critique

For the benefit of those who want to learn karate from this book without the aid of an instructor, a recommended training sequence is given below. Of course, the length of the practice sessions and the rigorousness of the training should be varied according to physical condition, age, etc. of the student.

Subject of training	Remarks
1. Introduction to karate	
2. Striking points	
3. Stance	Informal-attention stance, open-leg stance, forward stance
4. Posture	
5. Body shifting	From forward stance
6. Fore-fist straight punch	
7. Stance	Back stance
8. Body shifting	From back stance
9. Front kick	
10. Downward block	
11. Rising block	
12. Forearm block	
13. Basic sparring	Using only techniques studied so far, gradually adding new techniques as they are learned
14. Back-fist strike	
15. Bottom-fist strike	
16. Stance	Straddle-leg stance
17. Body shifting	From straddle-leg stance
18. Side kick	
19. Vertical-fist punch	
20. Close punch	
21. Knife-hand strike	
22. Ridge-hand strike	
23. Elbow strike	
24. Knife-hand block	
25. Roundhouse kick	

26. Semi-free one-blow sparring	Using only techniques learned so far, gradually adding new techniques as they are learned
27. Stance	Cat stance, diagonal straddle-leg stance
28. Palm-heel straight punch	
29. Roundhouse punch	
30. Hook punch	
31. Back-hand strike	
32. Palm-heel strike	
33. Punching block	
34. Back-hand block	
35. Bottom-fist block	
36. Back kick	
37. Stamping kick	
38. Flying front kick	
39. Techniques in combination	Using only techniques learned so far, gradually adding new techniques as they are learned
40. Freestyle sparring	
41. One-knuckle-fist straight punch	
42. Fore-knuckle-fist straight punch	
43. Spear-hand straight thrust	
44. Double-fist straight punch	
45. U-punch	
46. Augmented forearm block	
47. X-block	
48. Wedge block	
49. Scooping block	
50. Crescent kick	
51. Knee kick	
52. Inside snapping kick	
53. Crescent-kick block	
54. Formal exercise	Heian No. 4
55. Throwing techniques	
56. Self-defense	
57. Stance	Hourglass stance, wide hourglass stance
58. Rising punch	
59. Bent-wrist block	
60. Chicken-head-wrist block	
61. Ox-jaw-hand strike	
62. Hooking block	
63. Grasping block	
64. Sweeping block	
65. Flying side kick	

Training gym

Any level floor which will not injure the bare feet and does not create either too much sliding or too much friction will do. The ideal floor is of polished wood. The room should be well ventilated, with no furniture, and spacious enough to allow freedom of movement.

Practice uniform

Any suit of light material that permits freedom of body movement will suffice. It is better if the face, wrists, hands, calves, ankles, and feet are exposed.

6
Calisthenics

Calisthenics are an essential part of any athletic training, and this is especially true of karate, which requires maximum control over all mobile parts of the body. Karate calisthenics are divided into four types: limbering-up exercises, muscle-strengthening exercises, exercises for improving the wind, and reaction-time exercises.

Exercise Sequence

Calisthenics and actual practice are usually conducted in the following sequence: limbering-up exercises, wind and reaction-time exercises, practice of karate techniques, strengthening exercises, limbering-up exercises.

A typical Japanese karate team distributes its exercise time as follows:

Limbering up—5 minutes
Wind and reaction-time exercises—10 minutes
Karate techniques—2½ hours
Strengthening exercises—10 minutes
Limbering up—5 minutes

Of course, if the muscles are tired, less time is devoted to strengthening exercises and more to limbering up.

Limbering-up Exercises

Two basic principles underlying the use of strength in karate are as follows: the shorter the duration of time the muscles are tensed in performing a given technique, the stronger the technique will be; and the greater the number of muscles brought into play at the same time, the stronger the technique will be. Although some muscles are more easily tensed than others, every effort should be made to harmonize their contraction. The aim of limbering up is to tone up the muscles and thereby make them more controllable. You should limber up at the beginning and end of every karate training session.

1. Body loosening: Relax all body muscles, particularly arms and shoulders, and gently lift shoulders up and down.

2. Neck twisting: Twist head several times from left to right, then backward and forward; then bend neck left and right; finally, swing head in a wide circle.

3. Arm stretching (a): With shoulders relaxed, extend arms and rotate them in wide circles in front of the body, first in one direction, then in the other.

4. Arm stretching (b): Same as previous, except that arms are rotated to the sides of the body.

5. Side stretching: Be sure not to bend the body forward.

6. Trunk twisting: Be sure not to move feet. Twist as far as possible.

7. Trunk stretching: Be sure not to bend knees. Move the body in large circular motion and stretch as far as possible.

8. Back stretching: Do not bend knees.

9. Leg swinging: Swing legs as high as possible to the front and to the left and right. Do not lift heel of supporting leg; in swinging leg sideward, twist ankle and instep inward, so that the big toe points slightly downward.

10. Leg stretching: Stretch legs as shown, pushing knee joint down with hand.

11. Leg spreading: Spread legs as widely as possible.

12. Back stretching: Do not bend knees.

13. Leg relaxing : Gently vibrate legs and feet.

14. Joint loosening : Relax muscles and shake wrists and ankles.

Muscle-Strengthening Exercises

In general, the best exercise for developing and strengthening the muscles used in performing karate techniques is repeated practice of the techniques themselves. However, there are times when additional exercises to strengthen certain muscles or sets of muscles are required. Examples of some of these are given here. Of course, the amount and type of limbering-up and strengthening exercises should be varied according to body condition, limberness, and degree of muscular development. For example, if you are especially weak in kicking, leg limbering-up and strengthening exercises should be emphasized. If the muscles are tired and stiff after practice, strengthening exercises should be omitted in favor of limbering-up exercises.

Push-ups: Straighten arms and legs and raise hips upward, keeping heels flat on floor. Bending arms, lower the body close to floor; then repeat the first movement. Finally, keeping arms extended, lower the bottom half of the body. Repeat this sequence twenty or thirty times. This is a good all-around exercise for the arms, chest, abdomen, back, and ankles.

Pelvis twisting: Place hand on hips and twist hips in circular motion, first in one direction as far as possible, and then in the opposite direction. This strengthens the muscles of the hips and legs, especially those used in turning.

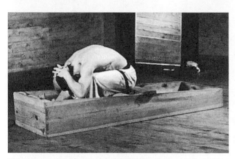

Trunk twisting: With legs held down, bend the upper part of the body backward and forward. Repeat, simultaneously twisting trunk sideways. This strengthens the side and front abdominal muscles.

Rabbit hopping: With hands clasped behind the back, bend the knees, lower the hips, and stand on the toes. Jump up and forward like a rabbit for a distance of about fifty yards. This exercise strengthens the muscles used in kicking and jumping.

Leg snapping: Lift leg so that thigh is parallel with the ground, then sharply snap the lower part of leg sideward. Repeat, snapping leg forward. This strengthens the muscles of the thighs, especially those used in the snap kick.

Leg lifting: Place hands on wall, lean body forward, and rapidly lift knee to chest. Do not lift heel of supporting leg. Repeat twenty-five times with each leg. This strengthens the hip muscles, especially those used in kicking.

Wind and Reaction-Time Exercises

There are many exercises for improving the wind and for sharpening reaction-time. Here are a couple of examples.

Ball punching: Left-hand punching, right-hand punching, and alternately left- and right-hand punching. This gives very good practice in timing.

Rope skipping: One jump per revolution, two jumps per revolution, and alternately one and then two jumps per revolution. This develops rhythmic movement of the entire body, builds lung capacity, tones up the elasticity of the body, and gives exercise in coordination.

PART 2
Basic Techniques and Their Practice

7
Striking Points and Vital Points

The principle behind all techniques in karate is the maximum concentration of the strength of the entire body for purposes of defense and attack. The striking points are the locations of these concentrations of strength. Theoretically, all hard surfaces of the body could be considered striking points, but only those parts and positions where the strength of the body can be concentrated easily are given here. These striking points are the true weapons of the karateka. Unlike other weapons, they cannot be bought ready-made, but must be forged on the anvil of individual training and discipline.

Fore-Fist (*seiken*)

The fore-fist is the most frequently used striking point in karate. It consists of the first and second knuckles of the forefinger and middle finger. Constant practice is necessary to produce and maintain a strong fore-fist.

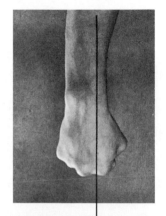

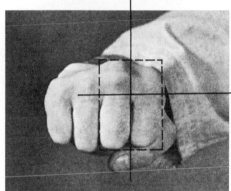

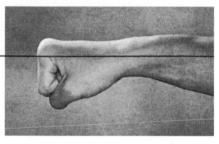

An imaginary straight line can be drawn from the center of the forearm to the point between the knuckles of the forefinger and middle finger.

The forearm and the knuckles form a straight line. Do not bend wrist. The top and front of the fist form a 90° angle.

The horizontal line represents a continuous straight line drawn through the center of the forearm and wrist. In order to convey the maximum

striking force of the body through the arm and wrist to the face of the fist, this line must be straight.

How to make a proper fist

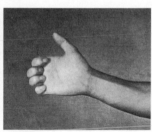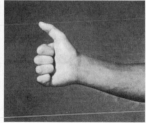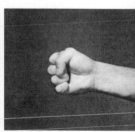

Starting with the little finger, tightly clench the fingers in succession; finally, press the forefinger and middle finger down firmly with the thumb.

Other Striking Points

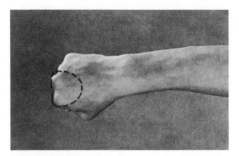

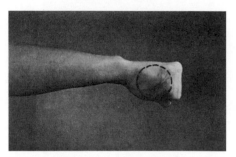

Back fist (riken): Used mainly in attacking the head, elbow joints, ribs, and other hard surfaces, and also in blocking.

Bottom fist (tettsui): Used in attacking the face and ribs, and also in blocking.

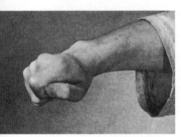

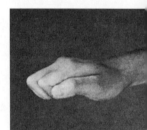

One-knuckle fist (ippon-ken): Extend knuckle of forefinger out from regular fist and hold down with thumb. Used in attacking the temple, between the eyes, and other minute vulnerable points.

Middle-finger one-knuckle fist (nakadate-ippon-ken): Same use as one-knuckle fist.

Fore-knuckle fist (hiraken): Press finger together with thumb. Used in attacking the point between nose and upper lip, temple, and solar plexus.

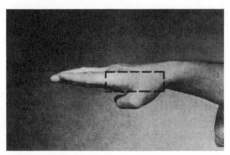

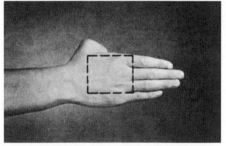

Ridge hand (haitō): Used in attacking the face, ribs, etc.

Back hand (haishu): Be sure to bend thumb down. Used in blocking and in attacking the ribs.

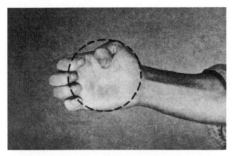

Bear hand (kumade): Used mainly in attacking ears, etc.

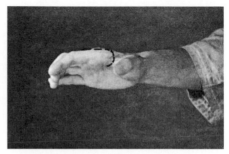

Tiger-mouth hand (kokō): Used in attacking the Adam's apple.

Two-finger spear hand (nihon-nukite): Used in attacking the eyes.

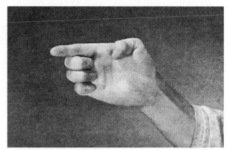

One-finger spear hand (ippon-nukite): Used in attacking the eyes and solar plexus.

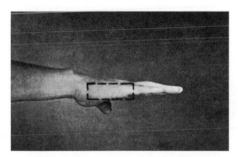

Knife hand (shutō): Press inward with thumb and little finger. Used mainly in blocking, but also in attacking the temple, neck, ribs, etc.

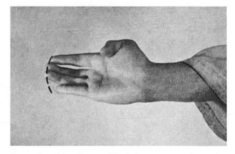

Spear hand (yonhon-nukite): Be sure to make ends of three striking fingers flush. Used in attacking the solar plexus, ribs, and chest.

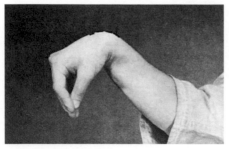

Bent wrist: Used mainly in blocking.

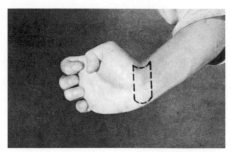

Palm heel (teishō): Bend wrist upward to form a nearly 90° angle. Used in attacking the face, nose, chin, jaw, solar plexus, and also in blocking.

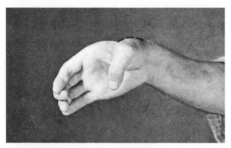

Chicken-head wrist (keitō): Used mainly in blocking.

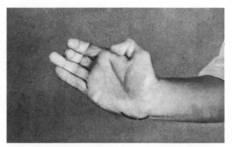

Ox-jaw hand (seiryūtō): Used mainly in blocking and in attacking the collarbone.

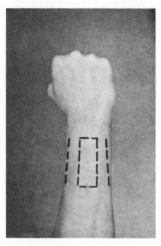

Forearm (ude): Used mainly in blocking, especially the part near the wrist. It is used in very strong blocking techniques. The outer, inner, and upper surfaces of the forearm are used.

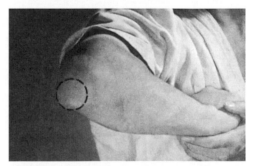

Elbow (empi): Used mainly in attacking the chin, chest, solar plexus, and ribs, and also in close-in blocking.

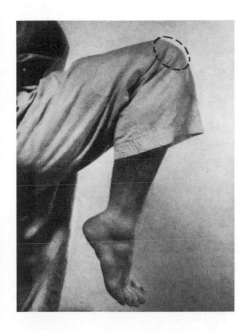

Knee (hittsui): Used in close-range attack to the face, solar plexus, groin, etc.

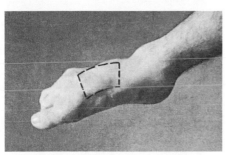

Instep (haisoku): Used in front and roundhouse kicking to attack the groin.

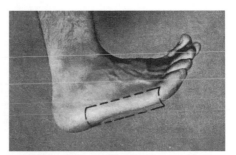

Foot edge (sokutō): Used in side kicking and stamping to attack the jaw, armpit, solar plexus, knee, etc.

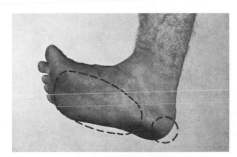

Sole (teisoku): Used in blocking and in crescent kicking to attack solar plexus.

Heel (kakato): Used in back kicking and stamping to attack the jaw, solar plexus, groin, instep.

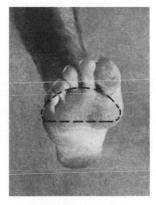

Ball of the foot (koshi): Be sure to curl toes upward as far as possible. Used in front and round-house kicking to attack the face, jaw, solar plexus, groin, ribs, etc.

Vital Points and their Respective Striking Points

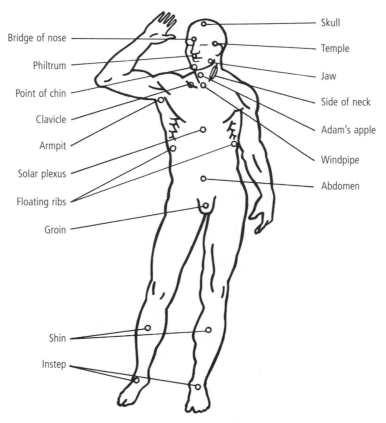

Bridge of nose
Philtrum
Point of chin
Clavicle
Armpit
Solar plexus
Floating ribs
Groin

Skull
Temple
Jaw
Side of neck
Adam's apple
Windpipe
Abdomen

Shin
Instep

Vital points	Striking points most commonly used	
	Hand	**Foot**
Skull	Bottom fist	
Bridge of nose	Fore-fist, back fist, one-knuckle fist, fore-knuckle fist, ridge hand, one-finger spear hand (esp. eyes), two-finger spear hand (esp. eyes)	
Temple	Fore-fist, back fist, bottom fist, ridge hand, one-knuckle fist, fore-knuckle fist, palm heel, bear hand (esp. ears)	Ball of the foot
Philtrum	Fore-fist, back fist, one-knuckle fist, fore-knuckle fist, ridge hand, palm heel	Foot edge, heel, knee (all of face)
Jaw	Fore-fist, palm heel	Ball of the foot, foot edge
Chin	Fore-fist, palm heel, elbow	Ball of the foot, foot edge, heel
Adam's apple	One-knuckle fist, fore-knuckle fist, tiger-mouth hand, one-finger spear hand, spear hand	
Windpipe	One-knuckle fist, one-finger spear hand	
Side of neck	Ridge hand, knife hand	Foot edge
Base of cerebellum	One-knuckle fist, fore-knuckle fist	Ball of the foot
Clavicle	Bottom fist, knife hand, ox-jaw hand	
Armpit	Fore-knuckle fist, elbow	Ball of the foot, foot edge, heel

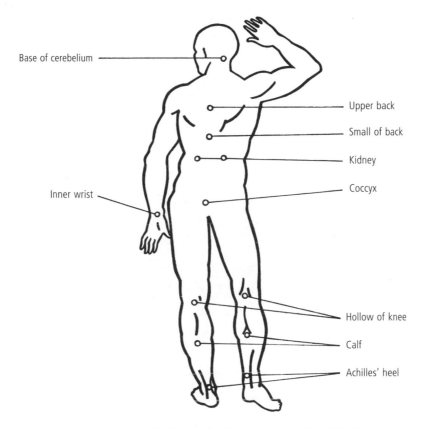

Base of cerebelium

Upper back

Small of back

Kidney

Coccyx

Inner wrist

Hollow of knee

Calf

Achilles' heel

Upper back	Fore-fist, back fist, bottom fist, fore-knuckle fist, palm heel, elbow	Ball of the foot
Solar plexus	Fore-fist, back fist, bottom fist, one-knuckle fist, fore-knuckle fist, spear hand, palm heel, elbow	Ball of the foot, foot edge, heel, sole, knee
Floating ribs	Fore-fist, back fist, bottom fist, one-knuckle fist, fore-knuckle fist, palm heel, elbow, back hand	Ball of the foot, foot edge, knee, heel
Small of back	Fore-fist, back fist, bottom fist, fore-knuckle fist, palm heel, elbow	Ball of the foot, heel, knee
Kidney	Fore-fist, back fist, bottom fist, one-knuckle fist, fore-knuckle fist, palm heel, elbow	Ball of the foot, foot edge, heel, knee
Abdomen	Fore-fist	Ball of the foot, foot edge, heel, knee, sole
Coccyx		Ball of the foot, foot edge, heel, knee
Groin	Knife hand, palm heel	Ball of the foot, foot edge, in-step, sole, knee, heel
Inner wrist	Fore-fist, back fist, one-knuckle fist, fore-knuckle fist, bottom fist	
Hollow of knee		Ball of the foot, foot edge, heel
Shin		Ball of the foot, foot edge, heel
Calf		Ball of the foot, foot edge, heel
Achilles' heel		Ball of the foot, foot edge, heel
Instep		Foot edge, heel

8
Stance

Stance is an important element in any sport, and in karate strong and well-executed techniques of both defense and attack depend to a large extent on a balanced and stable stance. The various stances in karate are based on the two factors of strength and agility.

Informal-Attention Stance (*heisoku-dachi*)

Stand straight naturally, with shoulders and legs relaxed.

Open-Leg Stance (*hachiji-dachi*)

Spread legs about shoulder width apart, toeing out slightly, with legs straight and body relaxed.

These two stances are not a direct part of any karate technique; rather, they are natural postures of everyday use. One of the aims of karate training is to enable the student to move into offensive or defensive maneuvers from these natural positions.

Straddle-Leg Stance (*kiba-dachi*)

With heels planted firmly on the ground and toes pointing straight ahead, spread legs a distance about twice the width of the shoulders and bend knees outward. Weight is distributed evenly on both legs. Tighten all muscles of the legs and hips.

Keep back straight and push chest out. Knees should be directly over big toes.

In this stance, if the legs are too close together, the center of gravity of the body will be too high and balance unstable. On the other hand, if the legs are too far apart, the muscles cannot be tensed properly, the stance is weakened, and speedy movement is hampered. These observations apply equally to the other stances shown in the following pages.

By holding the feet stationary and bending the knees outward, the legs act somewhat like bows under tension, with the direction of stress pointing inward. This is a strong stance, particularly with respect to sideways movement. This principle of the bow is used in other stances as well.

← *Direction of tension*

Direction of release ➡

Direction of tension of front knee

Direction of tension of rear knee

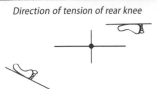

Forward Stance (*zenkutsu-dachi*)

Move one leg forward a distance about twice the width of the shoulders and about 30° to the side. The front leg should be bent at the knee and forced outward so that the knee is directly over the outer edge of the big toe. Keep the back straight and extend the rear leg fully. The toes of the front foot should point slightly inward. The front leg should bear 60 percent of the body weight and the rear leg 40 percent. Keep both feet flat on ground.

The forward stance is a strong stance to the front; therefore, it is used in attacking forward and in blocking attacks coming from the front.

Back Stance (*kōkutsu-dachi*)

Bend the rear knee and force it outward as in the straddle stance. Move the other leg out about twice the width of the shoulders, so that the front leg supports 30 percent of the body weight and the rear leg 70 percent. The directions of the feet form a right angle. Do not point the toes of the rear foot backward.

Because the front leg supports little of the body weight in this stance, it can be put into use easily, especially in kicking. By merely shifting the body weight without actually changing position, it is possible to close in on the opponent. Tensing the rear leg outward facilitates forward movement.

The rear knee should be slightly forward of the big toe.

Diagonal Straddle-Leg Stance (*sōchin-dachi*)

This is the straddle-leg stance twisted forward. The front knee is over the big toe, while the rear knee is about one foot forward of the big toe. The body weight is evenly distributed on both legs, and both knees are bent and tensed outward. Legs are about twice shoulder width apart; or seen from the front, shoulder width apart.

This is a strong stance both to the sides and front and to the rear, and is effective both in attack and defense. As in the straddle-leg stance, the bowing of the legs is very important.

Cat Stance (*neko-ashi-dachi*)

Tense the rear knee inward so that it points diagonally forward and is in a position slightly beyond the toes. With the rear foot flat on floor and bearing most of the body weight, raise the heel of the front leg and point the knee slightly inward. Keep the back straight.

Since the front leg bears practically none of the body weight, it is free for kicking. By moving into this stance from a wide-legged one, it is possible to keep a proper distance from the opponent. In order to obtain the maximum forward thrust, it is necessary to bend the rear knee and tense it as much as possible.

Hourglass Stance
(*sanchin-dachi*)

The knees are tensed inward, with the front knee directly over the toes and the rear knee about two inches forward of the toes. The toes point inward, and the body weight is evenly distributed. Rear toes and front heel are about even with each other, and the heels are about shoulder width apart.

This stance makes use of the tension of the legs bowed inward, the reverse of that in the straddle-leg stance. It provides thrust to the outside, which although not as strong as the opposite, does help mobility and moving into position for the next technique.

Directions of tension

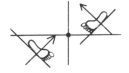

Wide Hourglass Stance
(*hangetsu-dachi*)

The wide hourglass stance is performed by spreading the legs twice the shoulder width.

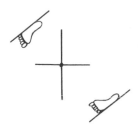

9
Posture

Without correct posture, it is impossible to perform karate techniques properly.

Front-Facing

Used mainly in attacking. Shoulders are parallel to target.

The basic posture in karate is where the upper part of the body is straight and perpendicular to the ground. In general, if the upper part of the body leans forward or to the side, balance is weakened, and correct techniques cannot be performed. However, there are a few rare exceptions where a non-vertical posture is called for. The three basic postures in karate are: front-facing, half-front-facing, and side-facing.

In every case, the upper part of the body is perpendicular to the ground.

Half-Front-Facing

Used mainly in defense. Shoulders face target at a 45° angle.

Side-Facing

Used in both attack and defense. Shoulders are perpendicular to target.

10
Body Shifting

Body shifting in karate consists of stepping, sliding, turning, or combinations of these.

The following points about body shifting should be memorized:
- Maintain strong balance at all times.
- Shift the weight of the body smoothly.
- Maintain correct posture at all times.
- Don't raise and lower hips more than necessary; they should move more or less in a straight line.
- Don't raise feet high off the ground; on the other hand, don't drag them either. In either case you will lose both speed and balance.

Stepping

Used with forward stance, diagonal straddle-leg stance, or back stance in shifting where a relatively large change of position is desired.

Stepping in from forward stance

The stepping foot should be raised only slightly off the floor. While moving the leg forward, keep it close to the inside to avoid exposing the groin to attack. Keep the stationary foot solidly on floor.

Stepping back from back stance

As above, keep the stationary foot solidly on floor.

Double-Stepping

When you want to cover a wide distance and at the same time move the upper part of the body smoothly so as to prevent the opponent from anticipating your moves, double-stepping is called for.

In double-stepping from the forward stance, the rear leg should be brought forward to a position slightly ahead of the body. Perform both steps smoothly, raising the feet only slightly off the floor. The hips should continue to face in the same direction throughout. Do not straighten the legs.

In double-stepping from the straddle-leg stance, the first foot is brought up even with and close to the other foot. Both steps must be performed smoothly, with the feet raised only slightly oft the floor. The body should continue to face in the same direction throughout. Be sure not to straighten the legs while stepping.

Sliding

This is used to cover short distances with agility.

To slide forward (e.g., from forward stance), without changing stance and using the forward thrust of the tensed rear leg, shift the front leg and body weight forward, allowing the rear leg to follow naturally.

To slide backward (e.g., from back stance), shift the entire body backward, taking care not to straighten the rear leg.

To slide sideways (e.g., from straddle-leg stance), maintain stance and shift the entire body smoothly sideways in one motion.

Slide-Stepping

Used in making larger position shifts than is feasible with sliding.

In slide-stepping forward (e.g., from forward stance), slide forward as shown on the previous page, and as the slide is completed, take one step forward. The shift from sliding to stepping must be performed smoothly. Be sure to maintain stance throughout.

In slide-stepping backward (e.g., from back stance), slide backward as shown on the previous page, and at the end of the slide, take one step backward smoothly. Be sure to keep a strong rear leg throughout.

Turning

To turn 180° from a forward stance, move the rear foot sideward about two shoulder widths and pivot around on the balls of the feet. Do not raise heels more than necessary. (When the front and rear leg are in a straight line, as in the back stance, the initial step is not necessary.)

Step-Turning

Used when a shift in position, as well as in direction, is desired.

Pivoting on the ball of the rear foot, swing the front foot around so as to resume the same stance in the opposite direction.

11
Hand Techniques

Along with foot techniques, hand techniques are the lifeblood of karate. They are used in both attack and defense for punching, striking, blocking, deflecting, etc. Here the various hand techniques are broken down into attacking techniques and defending techniques. Attacking techniques are further broken down into punching and striking; the respective basic techniques of each of these are fully explained in the following pages.

ATTACKING TECHNIQUES

The purpose of offensive techniques in karate is to render the attack of the opponent ineffective; therefore they are not used against an opponent whose attacks pose no threat. One of the unique features of karate is that attacking techniques can be used directly for blocking as well. This should be kept in mind in studying the following pages. The various forms of attacking by hand are broadly differentiated into punching and striking. The distinction between these will become clear from the examples shown.

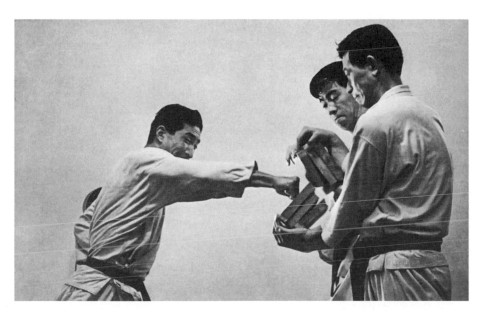

Punching Techniques

Punching techniques make use of the fore-fist, one-knuckle fist, fore-knuckle fist, palm heel, spear hand, etc. All the representative hand techniques based on the use of these striking points are both fast and effective.

In basic practice the punching hand should start from the ready position just above the hip bone, but for actual use it must be trained to punch smoothly and effectively from any position.

Fore-Fist Straight Punch (*seiken-choku-zuki*)

This is probably the most widely used technique in all of karate. It is extremely strong and speedy and effective when the distance to be covered is short. It is a straight outward thrust of the fist, which is twisted 180° simultaneously as it moves from the ready position to the target with the arm fully extended. It is useful for attacking the face, solar plexus, lower abdomen, etc.

Principle: According to karate theory, a vertical line drawn directly in front of the center of the body represents the area at which the greatest strength of the body can be concentrated. Whether aiming at the opponent's face or his stomach, the blow should strike in this area. Without unduly tensing the muscles of the shoulders and arms, the fist and elbow move directly toward the target in the shortest distance at the fastest speed. As the attacking arm moves out, the other arm is simultaneously pulled back to a ready position, adding more force to the punch. At the point of greatest extension of the attacking arm, all of the muscles of the body are stiffened, or "focused." This focus is momentary, and in the next instant the muscles are relaxed and preparations are made for the next punch.

- Practice this punch from the open-leg stance.
- Lower shoulders, relax body.
- Place punching hand above hip bone, with thumb up and elbow pointing straight behind.
- Stretch the other hand slightly in front of body.

- Thrust punching hand straight forward, rubbing the elbow lightly along the side.
- As elbow passes beyond body, twist arm and wrist so that the arm is straight at its point of maximum extension.

- Simultaneously twist and retract other arm to ready position with thumb up.
- At point of impact thumb of punching hand should be down ward.

The principle behind twisting the forearm inward just before completing the punch is this: the snap of the arm augments the speed of the punch; it makes tensing the arm and chest muscles easier at the moment of impact; the force of the twisting is added to the force of the thrusting out to increase the overall strength of the punch; and it stabilizes the direction of the punching force. The purpose of retracting the opposite hand simultaneously with punching is based on the principle of physics that to every action there is an opposite and equal reaction. Thus, the greater the force with which the hand is retracted, the stronger the punch of the opposite hand.

At the moment of impact, all of the muscles of the body, but particularly those of the chest and back, must be momentarily tensed.

*Here is shown how **not** to punch. The wrist is bent up, dissipating the force of the punch and making injury to the wrist possible. The fist is weakly formed, making a strong punch impossible. The shoulder of the punching arm is thrust outward and upward, ruining the balance and making it impossible to focus the body muscles at the point of impact.*

Practice methods: From the open-leg stance, punch alternately with the right and then with the left hand, aiming at the solar plexus or face of an imaginary opponent. This is called "empty punching"; as the most fundamental practice method of karate, it should be repeated often. Besides single punching, also practice double and triple punching, in which two or three punches are delivered with the left and right hands alternately in rapid succession.

Adaptations of the fore-fist straight punch

1. Reverse punch (*gyaku-zuki*): This consists of punching with the hand which is on the same side as the rear foot. It gains force by making maximum use of the forward twisting motion of the hips. This adaptation of the fore-fist straight punch is so basic and so often used that it is treated as an independent technique in karate. Because it is a forward attacking technique, it is usually used with stances which are strongest to the front; i.e., forward stance or diagonal straddle-leg stance (shown here).

It is simply a fore-fist straight punch performed from a forward stance, with the hips twisted in the direction of the punch. The point at which the hips are twisted to their maximum extent should coincide with the focusing of the body muscles at the point of impact.

• The body is in half-front-facing posture.	• Keep back straight. Twist hips smoothly. • The shoulders and trunk face directly forward.	• Do not raise heel of rear foot. • Tense whole body, particularly the legs, at point of impact.

Major points to be kept in mind:

- Since much of the power of the reverse punch depends on correct timing of the forward twisting motion of the hips, emphasize practice in synchronizing the twisting and punching.
- Do not lean forward; otherwise, the twisting of the hips is delayed and the punch weakened.
- Do not allow the elbow of the punching arm to flap out from body; otherwise, it is impossible to transfer the power of the hip movement to the fist.

Applications of the reverse punch:

- After blocking a kicking attack.

- Catching the opponent off guard.

Methods for practicing the reverse punch:
- Stand in one spot and repeat the reverse punch, being sure to bring the hand and hips back along exactly the same course that was followed in punching out.
- From the open-leg stance, in one smooth movement step into forward stance and perform a reverse punch. Move back into open-leg stance and repeat with the opposite hand.

2. Lunge punch (*oi-zuki*): This consists of a fore-fist straight punch in which the punching hand is on the same side as the leg which moves forward. The force of the body moving forward is used to give strength to the punch. Like the reverse punch, the lunge punch is treated as an independent technique. It is ordinarily used with stances strong to the front, i.e., the forward stance and diagonal straddle-leg stance. It is very effective in closing in on the opponent and delivering a sharp attack.

- Start step by bringing rear leg quickly toward front leg.
- As stepping foot passes sttionary foot, begin fore-fist straight punch. Keep stepping leg bent. Don't move hips up and down.
- Stretch stationary leg, thrust hips forward, and as stepping foot is planted down, simultaneously complete punch and focus body. Keep back straight. Don't lift heel.

Avoid these mistakes:

- Leaning the body forward; this will upset the balance, diminish the strength of the hips, and weaken the punch.
- Completing step before or after the punch is completed; the punch will not gain the extra strength derived from the force of the forward movement.
- Starting the punch too soon, then holding back to allow the leg to catch up: unless the punch is performed in one movement, it will be weak.
- Lifting the stepping foot too high or dragging it along the floor; doing either slows down the stepping and weakens the thrust of the hips.

Methods for practicing the lunge punch:

- From open-leg stance, step into the lunge punch, return to original position, and repeat with the opposite hand.
- Step forward in a straight line, lunge punching alternately with one hand and then the other.

- Occasionally throw in a reverse punch with the opposite hand immediately after completing the lunge punch. Another variation is to add a third punch after the reverse punch.

In all the above cases, the lunge punch should be practiced as an attack both to the face and to the solar plexus of an imaginary opponent.

Applications of the lunge punch:

- Moving in as the opponent advances.

- Breaking the opponent's stance.

Variations of the straight punch

In these three techniques, the striking points vary, but the basic principle and methods of use are the same as those for the fore-fist straight punch.

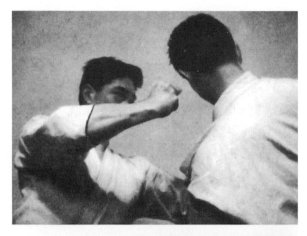

1. One-knuckle-fist straight punch (*ippon-ken-zuki*)

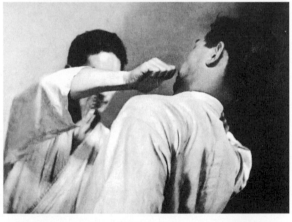

2. Fore-knuckle-fist straight punch (*hiraken-zuki*)

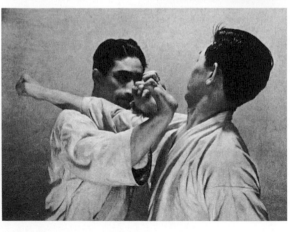

3. Palm-heel straight punch (*teishō-zuki*)

Spear-Hand Straight Thrust (*nukite*)

These spear-hand techniques are performed just like the fore-fist straight punch, except that the wrist and forearm are not twisted just before the point of impact.

Vertical spear-hand straight thrust

Horizontal spear-hand straight thrust

Two-finger spear-hand straight thrust

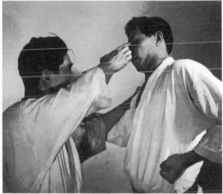

One-finger spear-hand straight thrust

Vertical-Fist Punch (*tate-zuki*)

In principle, this is like the fore-fist straight punch, except that the arm is twisted only a quarter turn and the punch is completed with the fist in a vertical position. Be sure to keep the elbow close in to the body. This is especially useful for a close-in attack.

Reverse-punch form

Lunge-punch form

Application: After closing in and blocking the opponent's attack.

Rising Punch (*age-zuki*)

This is a sweeping, rising punch used primarily for attacking an opponent's jaw. The striking fist describes a wide arc from the hip to the target. Rotating the fist inward, snap forearm and wrist from the elbow. Simultaneously retract the opposite hand to the hip. Be sure to keep the elbow close in to the body and do not bend the wrist. Focus the body muscles at point of impact.

Avoid this mistake: Raising the shoulder of the punching arm or thrusting it forward; these weaken the force of the punch and throw one off balance.

Adaptation: This technique is very much like the fore-fist straight punch and is used in more or less the same way. It may be performed both as a reverse punch and as a lunge punch.

Application: Dodging to the outside of the opponent's reverse-punch attack.

Roundhouse Punch (*mawashi-zuki*)

This is a circular punch aimed at the opponent's temple. The fore-fist, fore-knuckle fist, one-knuckle fist, etc. may all be used as the striking point. As soon as the elbow leaves the body, the fist describes an arc, and is simultaneously twisted inward 180°. Be sure to strike the target from the side but directly in front of the body. Focus strongly at point of impact.

Avoid this mistake: Swinging the body beyond a front-facing position; this interferes with focusing the punch and also puts one in an extremely vulnerable position.

Adaptation: This technique is usually performed as a reverse punch, to take advantage of the twisting movement of the hips, but may also be performed as a lunge punch.

Application: Dodging outside an opponent's lunge-punch attack, simultaneously grasping and pulling his sleeve.

Close Punch (*ura-zuki*)

This is an effective form of attack in close-in fighting and is delivered with the inside of the wrist up. It is especially important to keep the elbow close to the body. Give the wrist a twist outward just before focusing. Special emphasis should be given to tensing the chest muscles while focusing.

Avoid this mistake: Allowing the punching fist to swing up so that it strikes the target at an angle, rather than straight on.

Adaptation: This is performed both as a reverse punch and as a lunge punch. Since it is particularly effective when close to the opponent, it is often delivered from the straddle-leg stance.

Application: Shifting to the side and closing in on an attacking opponent.

Double-Fist Punch (*morote-zuki*)

This is a fore-fist straight punch in which both hands strike the same target at the same time. It is a powerful attacking technique which is difficult to block. (Shown is the regular double-fist punch; there is also a double-fist close punch.)

Avoid these mistakes:
- Lifting the shoulders up; this will make focusing difficult and weaken the punch.
- Leaning the upper part of the body forward; this also weakens the punch and throws one off balance.

Adaptation: This is usually executed from the forward or diagonal straddle-leg stance. It may be delivered in the lunge-punch form, with a step forward, or in the reverse-punch form, utilizing the twisting movement of the hips.

Application: Stepping inside an opponent's attacking arm.

U-punch (*yama-zuki*)

This is a simultaneous attack at the face with a fore-fist straight punch and at the solar plexus with a close punch. This is also a very difficult attack to block. It is especially useful against an opponent who has grabbed one's hair. In order for both fists to strike on a vertical line directly in front of the body, it is necessary to lean the body slightly forward and face directly forward. The chest muscles should be strongly tensed in focusing the punch. Do not lift up the shoulder of the arm aiming at the face, and do not push the buttocks out.

Avoid this mistake: Leaning the upper part of the body too far forward; this makes focusing difficult and destroys balance.

Adaptation: The U-punch is performed mainly from a forward or diagonal straddle-leg stance.

Application: A U-punch is delivered while simultaneously blocking opponent's attack to the face.

Hook Punch (*kagi-zuki*)

This is an effective technique for attacking from the side from close quarters. It is used with the fore-fist, fore-knuckle fist, one-knuckle fist, etc. to attack the temple, ribs, etc. As soon as the elbow passes the hip, the fist is twisted and thrust directly sideward in a sharp curve. Do not flap the elbow outward from the body. The point of impact should be directly in front of the opposite side of the body.

Adaptation: The hook punch is usually delivered from a forward, straddle-leg, or diagonal straddle-leg stance.

Application: Moving to close an outside opponent's punching attack.

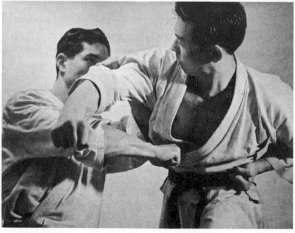

Striking Techniques

The Japanese make a clear distinction between punching and striking which may not be clear from the English words. Basically, the difference is like that between stabbing and slashing in the case of a sword. The force in a punch is transmitted in a straight line through the forearm to the striking point, whereas in striking the force is exerted laterally, usually with a snapping motion, particularly of the elbow. There are many striking techniques in karate, which are used not only for attack, but in many cases for blocking as well.

Back-Fist Strike (*riken-uchi*)

This is a technique which utilizes the snapping motion of the elbow to strike with the back of the fist. It is used mainly in close-in fighting as an attack to the face or solar plexus of the opponent. It can be performed either in a downward movement or a sideward movement.

1. Downward strike

Holding the elbow stationary, snap the fist downward. Twist the fist outward as the strike is completed. Be careful not to move the elbow backward beyond the side of the body. Retract the hand along the same line described in striking out.

Adaptations:
- From the straddle-leg stance, attack to the side.
- From the forward or diagonal straddle-leg stance, attack to the front.

Application:
Blocking a punching attack to the body.

2. Sideward strike

Aim the elbow at the target and, twisting the wrist, snap the fist sideward. The hand should move toward the target in a straight horizontal line.

Adaptation: The sideward back-fist strike is usually used to attack to the side, and is performed from the straddle-leg stance. It may also be performed from the forward or diagonal straddle-leg stance.

Application: Dodging and ducking a punching attack to the face.

Downward bottom-fist strike

Bottom-Fist Strike (*tettsui-uchi*)

This technique is performed in the same manner as the back-fist strike, except that the striking surface is the base of the fist. It may be performed downward or sideward to attack head, joints, and other hard surfaces, as well as face and solar plexus. A special advantage of this technique is that it presents little danger of injury to the attacking hand.

Sideward bottom-fist strike

←

Back-Hand Strike (*haishu-uchi*)

This technique is performed in the same manner as the back-fist strike, except that the fist is not clenched. It is used to attack the ears, solar plexus, etc. It can also be used as a blocking technique. It is especially important to snap the wrist outward at the completion of the strike.

It is usually performed from the straddle-leg stance to attack to the side.

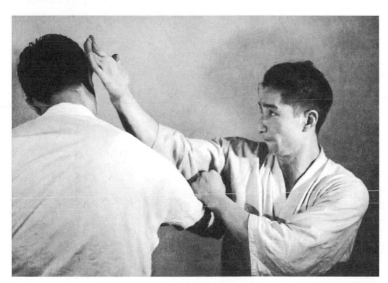

Knife-Hand Strike (*shutō-uchi*)

This is a striking technique in which the snapping force of the elbow and the twisting of the wrist are used in attacking opponent's neck, etc. with the edge of the hand.

1. Outside strike

Pass the hand smoothly to a point near the ear, with the elbow bent and pointing sideways. Swing the hand in a wide arc to the target. At the point of impact, the elbow should be in front of the body.

Avoid these mistakes:

- Not twisting the arm sufficiently so that the palm is not upward at moment of impact; this weakens the force of the blow.
- Raising the shoulder of the striking arm so that the chest muscles cannot be tensed; this also weakens the force of the blow.
- Not squeezing the fingers of the striking hand tightly together; this weakens the force of the blow and causes possible injury to the fingers.

Adaptation: The knife-hand strike may be performed from the forward or diagonal straddle-leg stance, either in the form of a lunge punch or a reverse punch. The latter is especially effective, since the force of the twisting of the hips is added to the strike.

Application: While blocking a punching attack.

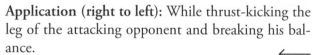

2. Inside strike

Raise the striking hand smoothly to a point near the opposite ear and swing forward in a wide arc to the target. Just before the point of impact, twist the arm so that the palm is downward, focusing at a point directly in front of the body.

Adaptation: This is performed in the same manner as the outside knife-hand strike. In this case, however, the force of the blow does not vary between the lunge-punch form and the reverse-punch form.

Application (right to left): While thrust-kicking the leg of the attacking opponent and breaking his balance.

Ridge-Hand Strike (*haitō-uchi*)

This technique, also, may be performed in two ways: from the inside and from the outside. It is used in attacking the ribs, temples, etc., and also in blocking. (See page 52 for striking point used.)

1. Outside strike
Swing the hand in a wide outside arc and snap it inward just before striking the target, so that the palm is downward and directly in front of body.

Avoid this mistake: Raising the shoulder of the striking arm or thrusting it forward; these actions make it impossible to tense the chest muscles and weaken the force of the blow.

Adaptation: This technique is usually performed from the forward or diagonal straddle-leg stance in either lunge-punch or reverse-punch form.

Application: Simultaneously dodging to the outside and blocking an attack to the solar plexus.

2. Inside strike

Swing the arm in an inside arc, snapping the hand upward just before the point of impact. Strike the target with the palm upward directly in front of the hips.

Avoid this mistake: Lifting the shoulder of the striking arm and not twisting the hand far enough, so that the target is struck at an angle.

Adaptation: This also may be performed from the forward or diagonal straddle-leg stance, and in the lunge-punch or reverse-punch form.

Palm-Heel Strike (*teishō-uchi*)

This may be performed in two ways: upward or from the side. It is used for attacking the face, chin, ribs, solar plexus, etc. and also for blocking.

1. Upward strike
From a point near the abdomen, thrust the hand in a straight line upward and outward from body, simultaneously twisting the hand outward. Keep the elbow close to the body. At the moment of impact, the heel of the palm points directly upward.

Avoid these mistakes:
- Lifting the shoulder of the striking arm.
- Not bending the wrist enough.

Adaptation: This is performed from the forward or diagonal straddle-leg stance in either the lunge-punch or reverse-punch form.

Application: While blocking an attack to the solar plexus.

2. Sideward strike

Swing the hand in a wide arc to the rear of the body and then to the side, simultaneously twisting the hand outward. Utilizing the snapping motion of the wrist, focus the blow so that the thumb is upward when the palm heel strikes the target. Be sure to bend the wrist sharply.

Avoid this mistake: Thrusting the hand directly sideways instead of in an arc; in this case the palm heel will strike the target at an angle and be ineffective.

Adaptation: This is usually performed from the straddle-leg stance to attack to the side, but it may also be used in attacking to the front from a forward or diagonal straddle-leg stance.

Application: Dodging outside an attack to the face.

Elbow Strike (*empi-uchi*)

This is a very powerful technique used mainly in close-in fighting. It can be broken down into four separate techniques: forward strike, upward strike, sideward strike, and backward strike. It is used mainly to attack the chin, solar plexus, or ribs of the opponent.

Avoid these mistakes:

- Lifting the shoulder of the striking arm; this makes it difficult to tense the chest muscles in focusing the strike.
- Swinging the elbow outward and moving it in an arc toward the target; this dissipates the strength of the strike and causes it to glance off the target.

1. Forward strike

Point the elbow at the target and strike outward in a straight line, twisting the wrist inward and bending the elbow deeply.

2. Upward strike

Keeping the arm close to the body, swing the elbow upward, twisting the hand inward and bending the elbow deeply so that the hand is close to the ear at the point of impact.

←

3. Sideward strike

Turning the wrist inward and bending the elbow deeply, strike directly sideward in a straight line.

←

4. Backward strike

Twist the hand outward and thrust the elbow straight backward. This strongly resembles the movement of the retracting hand in the forward punch. By round-house punching to the rear with the opposite hand, the technique is made stronger and more effective.

Adaptation: These techniques may all be performed from the forward or diagonal straddle-leg stance in the lunge punch or reverse punch form. As especially effective techniques in close-in fighting, they may be performed from the straddle-leg stance.

Application:

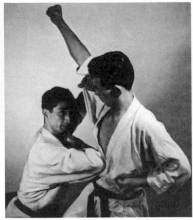

Forward strike

Sideward strike

Upward strike

Backward strike

BLOCKING TECHNIQUES

The true art of karate is said to begin and end with blocking. Another motto is: "In karate, never make the first move." The meaning behind both of these expressions is that karate ethics oppose its use for offensive purposes.

Since karate originated and has developed as an art of self-defense, blocking techniques are highly developed. Most of these are performed with the hands, in which the opponent's attacking hand or foot is struck, deflected, pressed down, hooked, or in some other way blocked, so that the attack is rendered ineffective. A distinctive feature of many karate blocking techniques is that they are "focused" blocks, in which the whole strength of the body is concentrated at the blocking point and then withdrawn. The advantage of this is that they often inflict such pain on the opponent's attacking arm or leg that he is discouraged from attacking again. Also, this kind of block enables one to maintain posture and balance and be immediately ready to perform the next technique, be it a counterattack or another block.

In karate, the blocking technique to be used in any given situation must be determined on the basis of the form of attack, the strength of the opponent, one's own position in relation to that of the opponent, one's own strength, and other pertinent factors. The following points, particularly, should be borne in mind:

- Make every effort to turn the opponent's strength to your own advantage.
- Be sure to maintain your own balance and posture in blocking.
- The blocking hand should not be over-engaged in the block, but should be preparing for the next technique.
- While blocking and afterward, be sure your posture or position does not offer your opponent an opening.
- While blocking, you should have in mind the counterattack you will follow up with.

Rising Block (*age-uke*)

This is a widely used focused block consisting of raising the arm and striking the attacker's arm with the outer surface of the forearm near the wrist. It is usually used to block an attack to the face.

    With the elbow bent about 90°, swing the arm upward, keeping it close in to the body. As the arm passes in front of the body, twist it inward, then snap it upward and focus at a point about three inches out from the top of the forehead. At this point the thumb should be downward. The point of contact should be directly in front of the vertical center of the body. Simultaneous with the upswing of the blocking arm, cross the opposite hand in front of the mouth and withdraw it strongly to the ready position.

Avoid these mistakes:
- Lifting the shoulder of the blocking arm; this makes it difficult to tense the muscles of the chest and weakens the block.
- Raising the elbow to a point higher than the blocking hand; this will weaken the technique to the extent that it will be ineffective in blocking the attack.
- Swinging the elbow beyond the side of the body; this makes it difficult to concentrate the strength of the body at the point of impact.
- Completing the block at a point too far away from the body; this provides the opponent with an opportunity to attack again with the same arm.

Adaptation: Since this technique is used mainly to block attacks coming from the front, it is performed from those stances which are strong to the front, i.e., the forward or diagonal straddle-leg stance. The upper part of the body should be in the half-front-facing posture. The photographs to the right illustrate the use of the rising block while stepping back into a forward stance from a natural stance.

Application: As the opponent attacks with a reverse punch to the face.

An example of the additional use of the withdrawing hand: Ordinarily, the withdrawing hand is used to add force to the technique of the opposite hand. However, it can be used in other ways; for example, to pull the opponent into a punch from the other hand. Shown below is its use with the rising block: grasp the wrist of the opponent's attacking arm with the withdrawing hand and, while pulling it down, block upward with the other arm at the opponent's elbow joint, breaking his arm.

Forearm Block (*ude-uke*)

This is a strong defensive focused technique used to block an attack to the solar plexus and occasionally to the face. There are two kinds of forearm blocks: from the outside, in which case the striking point is the outer surface of the forearm near the wrist; and from the inside, with the inner surface of the forearm near the wrist as the striking point.

Avoid these mistakes:
- Blocking with the elbow in a position not in front of the body; this prevents tensing the muscles of the chest, making the block ineffective.
- Unbending the arm too much, as this leaves the body open for further attack; the elbow should be bent at an angle between 80° and 90°.
- Not twisting the hand of the blocking arm far enough; this results in not striking with the proper blocking surface, weakening the block.

1. Outside block
With the elbow bent, swing the forearm from a point near the ear to the front of the body. Snap the fist outward and focus strongly at the point of impact. At the completion of the block, the elbow should be in front of the body and not to the side.

2. Inside block
With the arm bent and the fist near the opposite armpit, swing the forearm to the front of the body, twisting the hand outward and using the elbow as if it were a fulcrum. Focus strongly at the point of impact. Be sure that the elbow does not move beyond the front of the body.

Adaptation: These blocking techniques are usually performed from the forward or diagonal straddle-leg stance and in the lunge-punch or reverse-punch form. They are also occasionally performed from the straddle-leg stance.

Applications:
An outside block of a punching attack to the solar plexus.

An inside block of a punching attack to the face.

Moving into an attack: There are many ways of counterattacking after executing the forearm block. Below is an example of counterattacking with an elbow strike immediately following an outside forearm block.

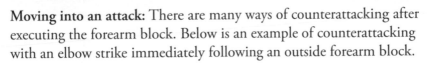

Knife-Hand Block (*shutō-uke*)

This speedy block is a technique unique to karate. It is used in a wide range of situations, mainly to defend against an attack to the solar plexus. However, beginners often experience difficulty in performing it properly. The special advantage of this block is that it puts one in a "ready" position for immediate counterattacking or for further defense.

Start with the blocking hand beside the opposite ear, and with the elbow as a fulcrum, slash the forearm down diagonally, simultaneously twisting the hand inward. At the same time, quickly pull the withdrawing hand, unclenched, to a position in front of the middle of the chest, with the palm upward. Take special care to attain the correct angle with the blocking arm and the correct position of the elbow at the point of focusing the block.

Avoid these mistakes:
- Lifting the shoulder of the blocking arm; this makes it difficult to tense the chest muscles in focusing the block.
- Straightening the arm too much or moving elbow outward away from body; these actions will render the block ineffective.
- Bending the wrist or moving the arm in an arc rather than a straight line; these actions will also weaken the block.

Adaptation: Since this technique is for the most part made use of while shifting to the rear, it is most conveniently performed from the back stance. Shown on the right is the knife-hand block being performed while stepping back from an open-leg stance into a back stance. Note that the upper part of the body assumes a half-front-facing posture.

Application: Stepping back from a punching attack . . .

. . . and, after blocking, counterattacking with the front leg from the back stance.

Application:
Confronted with a
kicking attack.

(Note that the right
hand of the man who
has blocked is moving in
for the counterattack.)

Downward Block (*gedan-barai*)

This is a technique which uses the outer surface of the forearm near the wrist to deflect and block an attack to the solar plexus, the abdomen, or the groin. It is especially effective in defending against kicking attacks. After completing the block, one is in a standard "ready" position.

Swing fist of blocking hand from a point near the opposite ear diagonally downward in a strong deflecting motion, simultaneously twisting arm so that wrist is downward. At point of impact, arm is fully extended. Be sure not to swing arm beyond the front of the body.

Avoid these mistakes:
- Lifting the shoulder of the blocking arm; this makes it impossible to tense the muscles of the chest.
- Failing to focus the block at the point of contact; this makes it ineffective as a block and destroys the balance.
- Failing to clench the fist of the blocking hand strongly enough; this makes it easy to injure the wrist.

Adaptation: Since this is a strong block against an attack from the front, it is usually performed from the forward or diagonal straddle-leg stance. Occasionally, it is used to defend against an attack from the side, in which case it is performed from the straddle-leg stance.

Augmented Forearm Block (*morote-uke*)

This technique is used in much the same way as the inside forearm block, but it is somewhat stronger, and after blocking one is in a "ready" position and can immediately move in to the counterattack or defend against a further attack.

This technique is performed in the same manner as the inside forearm block, except that the strength of the block is increased by swinging the opposite arm sharply in front of the body, instead of withdrawing it to the side. Bring the fist of the augmenting arm close to the elbow of the blocking arm, twist outward, and focus strongly at point of impact. This position makes it possible to tense the chest muscles and the muscles of both arms in focusing the block, giving it much extra strength.

Moving into an attack: A punching attack is blocked with an augmented forearm block; then the blocking hands are quickly exchanged and a reverse-punch counterattack delivered with the original blocking hand.

X-block (jūji-uke)

This is an effective blocking technique which requires comparatively little strength and which can be easily turned to one's advantage in counterattacking. There are two types of X-blocks: blocking upward to defend against an attack to the face; and blocking downward to defend against a kicking attack to the abdomen or groin.

1. Upward block

Thrust both hands in a straight line upward so that they cross at a point even with the top of the head and about one foot away. The purpose of leaving the hands open is to facilitate grasping or twisting the opponent's wrist in counterattacking. Right-handed persons should ordinarily place the left hand in front of the right.

Avoid these mistakes:
- Thrusting the elbows outward beyond the sides of the body; this weakens the block so that it will give way under the impact of a strong attack.
- Moving the hands in an outside arc in front of the body instead of in a straight line; this weakens the block, since they will not make contact with the attacking arm at a right angle; if anything, move hands in an inside arc from the chest outward.

Adaptation: Since this technique is most effective in blocking an attack from the front, it is usually performed from the forward or diagonal straddle-leg stance, but since comparatively little strength is required, it can also be performed from a kneeling or sitting position.

Applications: Moving into an attack from upward block.

Grasping and pulling opponent's arm while delivering front kick.

Twisting opponent's arm against the joint and attacking to the face.

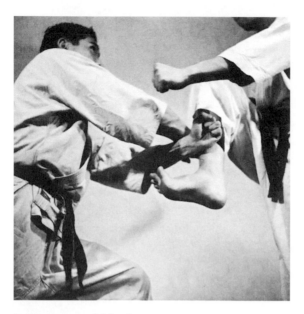

2. Downward block

Cross fists near one side of the body and thrust them strongly downward so that they strike at a point in front of the abdomen about one foot away. Right-handed people usually perform this technique from the right side, with the right hand over the left. Unlike the upward block, in this case the fists are tightly clenched to avoid injury to the fingers in blocking a strong kick.

Avoid these mistakes:
- Leaving the elbow bent or projecting beyond the side of the body; this weakens the block so that it cannot withstand the shock of a strong attack.
- Merely pressing down with the crossed fists without focusing; this also weakens the block and makes it impossible to prepare for the next technique.
- Leaning the upper part of the body forward; this destroys one's balance.

Adaptation: This technique is usually performed from stances strong to the front; i.e., the forward and diagonal straddle-leg stances.

Timing of downward block: To insure that the block will be effective, every effort should be made to block a kicking attack in its initial stages. Therefore, special attention should be paid to timing.

Wedge Block (*kakiwake-uke*)

This is a double-handed block in which the outer surfaces of the wrists are used to block a double-fist punch or to defend against an opponent who attempts to grasp one's lapels.

Place both fists in front of the face, with knuckles outward and elbows pointing downward. With the elbows as a fulcrum, snap the wrists down and outward to complete the block, focusing at the point of contact.

Avoid these mistakes:
- Thrusting elbows beyond sides of body; this weakens the block and makes it ineffectual.
- Straightening the arms too much; this also weakens the technique.

Adaptation:
This technique is usually performed from the forward or diagonal straddle-leg stance, but in order to be able to make an immediate kicking counterattack, it is often performed from the back stance as well.

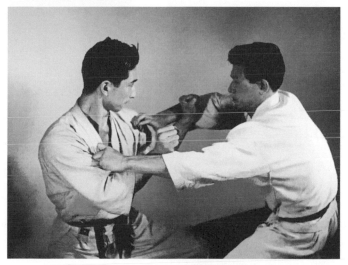

Application:
Upon being grasped by the lapels, step back into back stance and counterattack with a front kick.

Other Miscellaneous Blocks

The most basic techniques have been described in the foregoing pages. In addition, there are many others, the most common of which are described below and in the next three pages.

Punching block (*tsuki-uke*)
This is actually a punching attack and a block performed in one movement. With the arm slightly curved to ward off the opponent's attack with the outside surface of the arm, a fore-fist straight punch is delivered to the face.

Palm-heel block (*ō-uke*)
This is a speedy technique using the palm-heel strike (page 98) as a block against an attack to the face or solar plexus. It may be performed in three ways: by striking downward, upward, or from the side.

Chicken-head-wrist block (*keitō-uke*)

This is an upward block making full use of the snapping motion of the wrist. It is a speedy technique involving a minimum of motion. After blocking, by using the reverse snap and the ox-jaw hand (page 54) as the striking surface, block downward or counterattack to the opponent's collarbone.

Bent-wrist block (*kakutō-uke*)

This technique uses a wrist-snap similar to that of the chicken-head block. For an immediate counterattack, you can use the opposite snapping of the wrist to deliver a palm-heel strike.

Back-hand block (*haishu-uke*)

This is simply the back-hand strike used as a block, mainly against an attack to the solar plexus. The chief advantage of this technique is that, after blocking, it is easy to grasp the opponent's arm and pull him off balance.

Bottom-fist block (*tettsui-uke*)
This is the bottom-fist strike (page 92) used as a block. It is particularly effective as a strong block against the elbow or other hard surfaces of the opponent's attacking arm or leg.

Hooking block (*kake-uke*)
This technique is performed by sharply bending the elbow and swinging the forearm backward to a point near the ear, hook-blocking the opponent's attacking arm with the wrist. The advantages of this technique are that it requires a minimum of effort and it is possible while blocking to attack simultaneously with the opposite hand.

Grasping block (*tsukami-uke*)
This is performed by seizing the opponent's sleeve or pant leg, diverting the force of his attack and breaking his balance.

Sweeping block (*nagashi-uke*)

The force of the opponent's attack is literally swept aside with the palm or wrist. This technique allows one to block and simultaneously move in for the counterattack without expending a great deal of energy.

Pressing block (*osae-uke*)

This is similar to the sweeping block, except that the opponent's arm is pressed down and the counterattack delivered simultaneously. This technique is used mainly for blocking an attack to the abdomen or groin.

Scooping block (*sukui-uke*)

This technique consists of scooping the opponent's attacking leg with the forearm and strongly breaking his balance.

12
Foot Techniques

In karate, the feet as well as the hands are important weapons. In no other combative sport are the feet so rigorously or subtly trained; this is a unique feature of karate. Even without special training we are inclined to use our feet both for attack and defense, but with training they can be made into much more powerful weapons. In ordinary circumstances we do not use our feet in a large variety of ways, as we do our hands. Therefore, constant practice is necessary if they are to be made into effective weapons. It should be borne in mind that, like all karate techniques, not just the feet but the whole body must be used in the performance of foot techniques.

ATTACKING TECHNIQUES

Most foot attacking techniques—for that matter, most foot techniques—consist of kicking. There are three kinds of kicking techniques: snap-kicking, thrust-kicking, and striking, each of which has its own special advantage depending on the needs of the situation.

In kicking, special attention must be paid to the stationary foot, shifting of balance, and withdrawal of the kicking foot. Since the stationary foot must bear the entire weight of the body, it must be in a strong stance, particularly in the direction of the kick, if it is to withstand the shock of the kick striking the target. Balance must be shifted in such a way that the kicking leg bears none of the weight of the body, and at the same time this weight must be thrust in the direction of the kick to give it striking force. After the kick, the kicking leg must be quickly and smoothly withdrawn to avoid having it grabbed by the opponent and to allow for preparation for the next technique.

Front Kick (*mae-geri*)

The striking surface in the front kick is the ball of the foot. There are two kinds of front kicks: the snap kick, which makes use of the snapping motion of the knee to kick the opponent's jaw, armpit, solar plexus, or groin; and the thrust kick, in which the ball of the foot is thrust in a straight line to the target, much like a punch, to attack, for example, the opponent's abdomen.

Avoid these mistakes:

- Bending the back and extending the hips backward; this destroys balance and prevents the body from absorbing the shock of the impact; the kick is weakened without the thrusting forward of the hips.
- Not raising the knee high enough up to the chest; unless the kicking foot is raised at least as high as the knee of the supporting leg, the kick turns into a sort of shovelling motion, neither a snap or a thrust kick; also, the kicking leg should be bent as sharply as possible.
- Not kicking directly to the front of the body; balance is weakened and efficient use of the maximum number of body muscles is impaired.
- Lifting the heel or straightening the knee of the supporting leg; this weakens balance and control.
- Lowering the kicking leg to the ground without first withdrawing the knee to the chest (a very common mistake); this creates an opportunity for the opponent to grab the leg and also weakens balance and delays preparation for the next technique.

1. Front snap kick (*mae-geri-keage*)

Bend the kicking leg sharply, and lift the knee high and close to the chest. At the same time, bend the toes and ankle upward as much as possible and hold them there under tension. The knee muscles of the kicking leg should be relaxed and the ankle and knee of the stationary leg bent slightly, tensed, with the toes pointing in the direction of the target. The knee and toes of the kicking leg should be in a vertical straight line, with both pointing toward the target. Utilizing a snapping motion of the knee, kick upward directly in front of body, striking the target with the ball of the foot. Allow the kicking leg to return to the previous position with the knee next to the chest, and then lower to the original stance. Of course, all these actions should be performed in one smooth, continuous movement, not jerkily, so that the momentum of the first movement raising the knee to the chest adds force to the snapping motion of the kick. (**Note:** Occasionally, in making a front snap kick to the groin, the ankle is bent down and the kick delivered with the instep as the striking surface.)

2. Front thrust kick (*mae-geri-kekomi*)

Begin by raising the knee to the chest as in the snap kick, but rather than snapping the foot upward, thrust it outward in a straight line to the target; then withdraw the knee to the starting position and return to the original stance. When using the ball of the foot as the striking surface, the ankle should be bent slightly forward. When the heel is used as the striking surface, the ankle should be bent strongly backward. In learning this kick, it is better to practice the latter form, since it gives practice in extending the leg fully.

Adaptations:

The front kick may be performed from a stationary position with either the front or the rear leg, or it may be performed while moving forward. Shown here is an example of kicking with the rear leg while moving forward from a forward stance. The upper part of the body should be kept erect and the supporting leg planted firmly on the ground.

Shown below is an example of kicking with the front leg from a back stance, without moving forward. Note that the outward-bowing tension of the rear leg should be firmly maintained.

Side Kick (*yoko-geri*)

This technique uses the edge of the foot as the striking surface in a kicking attack to the side. There are two kinds of side kicks: one utilizing the snapping motion of the knee to kick upward; the other a thrust kick in which the foot is thrust out in a straight line like a punch. The former is generally used to attack the armpits, groin, jaw, etc. The thrust kick is used to attack the face, neck, solar plexus, ribs, thigh, etc.

Avoid these mistakes:

- Leaning the body too far in the opposite direction from the kick; this makes it impossible to transmit the strength of the body to the kicking foot.
- Pointing the toes of the kicking foot upward; the edge of the foot will not strike the target and the toes can easily be injured.
- Lifting the heel of the supporting leg off the ground or pointing the toes away from the kick; this weakens the kick.
- Kicking diagonally in front of the body, instead of directly to the side; this prevents the strength of the body from being transmitted to the kicking leg.
- Not lifting the leg or bending the knee sufficiently; this prevents the effective use of the snapping motion of the knee or the thrusting movement of the thigh.

The preparatory position is the same as that for the front kick, with the knee bent and raised in front of the body.

Side Snap Kick (*yoko-geri-keage*)

To perform the snap kick, utilize the snapping motion of the knee joint to jerk the foot sideways in an upward arc. At the beginning of the kick the knee should point diagonally toward the target. As the kick is completed, twist the hip inward and point the knee directly forward. Bend the ankle inward and point the toes downward, so that the edge of the foot strikes the target. As in the front kick, this technique should be performed in one smooth movement, so that the initial lifting of the knee gives force to the side-snapping motion.

Side Thrust Kick (*yoko-geri-kekomi*)

Aim the edge of the foot at the target and thrust sideways in a straight line. Quickly withdraw the kicking leg to the bent-knee position in front of the body and then return to original stance.

Adaptations:

The side kick in karate can be performed from any stance, but in almost every case the position shown in #5 is assumed before executing the kick. In the case of the straddle-leg stance illustrated in #1, the #5 position can be assumed directly and the kick completed, or first a double-step (page 68) can be taken and then the #5 position assumed. In the case of the forward stance illustrated in #3 or the back stance in #4, the #5 position is assumed directly.

In every case, the kicking leg should be withdrawn strongly, as shown in #7. Then, in most cases, the foot is lowered into the straddle-leg stance (the #1 position). However, it may be necessary on certain occasions to move directly into some other stance.

Supporting leg: In the front kick, it is fairly easy to tense the knee and ankle of the supporting leg to maintain a strong stance, but this position is not effective for the side kick, which requires a stance strong to the side. In order for the side kick to be effective, the supporting leg must be bowed outward as in the straddle-leg stance. This position exerts force in the direction of the kick and should be maintained throughout the kick.

Adaptations:

Shown above is a side snap kick to the armpit, passing under the opponent's arm in the guard position.

Dodging to the outside of opponent's attack, a side thrust kick is delivered to the side of his face.

Dodging to the inside of opponent's punching attack, a side snap kick is delivered to his chin.

Back Kick (*ushiro-geri*)

This technique uses the heel as the striking surface in attacking to the rear. Just as in the front and the side kick, there are two kinds of back kicks—the snap and the thrust. The former is used mainly to attack the groin or abdomen; the latter the stomach, face, etc.

Back snap kick (*ushiro-geri-keage*)

Back thrust kick (*ushiro-geri-kekomi*)

Similar to the preparatory position in the front kick, the knee is raised toward the chest and the ankle bent upward. Bending the supporting leg slightly more than for the front kick and keeping your eye on the target to the rear, swing the thigh backward and utilize the snap of knee to strike target with heel. Quickly withdraw the leg to the ready position and resume the original stance. To perform the thrust kick, thrust heel in a straight line to target; then quickly withdraw to ready position and return to original stance.

These kicks should be performed in one smooth movement, not jerkily. The supporting leg should exert strength in the direction of the kick, i.e., to the rear.

Avoid these mistakes:
- Leaning too far forward away from the direction of the kick; this weakens balance.

- Kicking diagonally to the rear rather than straight backward; this prevents putting the maximum strength of the body into the kick.
- Moving the body forward, away from the direction of the kick, while kicking; this will make the technique ineffective.

Adaptation: As with the other kicking techniques, the back kick can be performed from any stance, but in every case the ready position must be assumed before kicking. It is especially important to withdraw the kicking leg strongly and resume a strong stance. Shown above is the back kick being performed while moving backward from the forward stance. By twisting the hips sharply while withdrawing the kicking leg, a forward stance facing the opponent can be achieved. This is the most basic way to perform the back kick.

Applications:
Back-kicking an opponent who has tried to grab from behind.

A back thrust kick to the solar plexus of an opponent who has made a kicking attack.

Roundhouse Kick (*mawashi-geri*)

This is a technique in which the snapping motion of the knee and the swinging of the hips are utilized simultaneously to attack an opponent to the front with the ball of the foot. It may be used to attack the temple, neck, ribs, etc. Occasionally the roundhouse kick is used to attack an opponent on the left or right with the opposite foot.

Bending the ankle and knee sharply, lift the kicking leg up sideways. Swing the hips and snap the knee forward so that the foot moves in a circular motion to strike the target directly in front of the body. For a high kick, at the point of impact the foot should have passed its highest point so that the force of the kick points slightly downward, with the toes pointing slightly downward. The knee and ankle of the supporting leg should be slightly bent, with the foot flat on the floor and the toes pointing slightly beyond the target. At the completion of the kick, snap the leg back to ready position and resume original stance.

Avoid these mistakes:
- Allowing the body to swing too far; this weakens balance and makes it impossible to focus the kick on the target.
- Not returning the kicking leg to the ready position after kicking; this results in weakening posture to the opponent's advantage. For this reason, it is important that the toes of the supporting leg point almost directly forward.
- Swinging the leg forward without having bent the knee; this prevents the effective use of the knee snap, and the kick is weakened as a result.
- Bending the body too far away from kick; this weakens balance. Try to keep body as straight as possible.

- Not bending the ankle enough and allowing the toes to point upward at point of impact; this makes the ball of the foot glance off the target and creates the danger of injury to the toes.
- Not lifting the bent leg upward to the side before kicking; this makes the technique ineffective.

Adaptation: To perform the roundhouse kick from any stance or posture, the ready position must first be assumed and returned to afterward. Shown above is an example of the technique being performed from the forward stance, with the body moving forward.

Application: Simultaneously blocking a punching attack and attacking with a roundhouse kick to the neck.

Crescent Kick (*mikazuki-geri*)

This technique uses the sole of the foot as the striking surface to attack in a wide circular motion a target to the front or to the side opposite the kicking leg. It is used to attack the solar plexus, ribs, etc. and is also used widely as a block.

Lift the leg, slightly bent at the knee, and with a swivel-like movement of the hips swing the foot in an arc to the target, focusing in front of the body with the leg still slightly bent. At point of impact the toes should be pointing upward and the target struck with the flat sole of the foot. Withdraw the leg to a bent position in front of the chest and then resume original stance. During this kick, the toes of the supporting leg should point directly forward.

Avoid these mistakes:
- Swinging the body or the leg too far; this weakens balance and prevents effective focusing of the kick.
- Raising the heel of the supporting leg or leaning the body backward; this upsets the posture and weakens the force of the kick.

Application: Blocking a punching attack with a back-hand block, then counterattacking with a crescent kick to the solar plexus.

Adaptation: The crescent kick may be performed from any posture or stance, but it is most commonly used from the forward or straddle-leg stance. Below is a basic method of practicing the technique. The open hand to be extended to the side of the body as a target to kick at. As the kick is completed the body is moved forward and rotated so that one ends up facing in the opposite direction from the starting position. Be sure to focus the kick directly in front of the body.

Stamping Kick (*fumikomi*)

This technique is a downward kick either to the front, to the rear, to the inside, or to the outside. In the front and rear stamping kick, the heel is most commonly used as the striking surface. In stamp-kicking to the side, either inside or outside, the foot edge is mainly used. Stamping is chiefly used to attack the opponent's knee joint, shin, ankle, instep, etc. It may also be used to block or press down the foot of an attacking opponent.

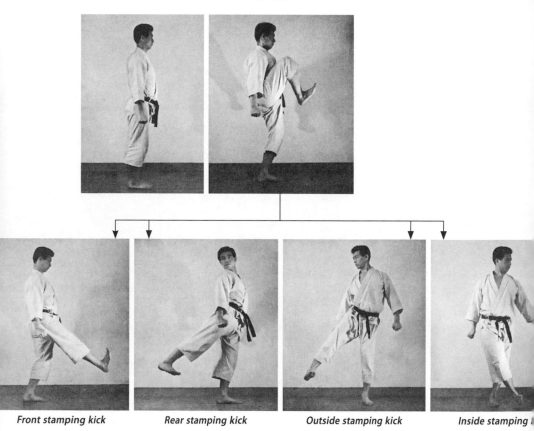

Front stamping kick   Rear stamping kick   Outside stamping kick   Inside stamping

With the ankle bent upward, lift the knee high toward the chest and thrust the foot downward in a straight line to the target, whether to the front, to the rear, or to the sides. After the kick is completed, lift the knee to ready position and then resume original stance.

In stamp-kicking to the front or rear, the foot should not extend beyond an imaginary line drawn through the center of the body. Similarly, in stamp-kicking to the side, the foot should not extend behind a line drawn sideways through the body. The shock of impact of these stamping techniques must be absorbed upward, so a strong posture and stance are essential.

Applications:
Front-stamping the instep of attacking opponent.

Rear-stamping the instep of an opponent
who attempts to grab from behind.

Outside-stamping an opponent's knee joint, throwing
him off balance.

Inside-stamping an opponent's knee joint,
throwing him off balance, and preparing
to deliver a punching attack.

Flying Front Kick (*mae-tobi-geri*)

In karate there are techniques involving jumping into the air and kicking once, twice, or three times. The double kick is the most common of these. The primary use of the flying kick is as a surprise attack to the solar plexus, chin, or face. A common adaptation is to kick aside the opponent's guarding hand with the first leg and to attack his chin with the second.

Starting from the forward stance, front snap kick with the left leg (in this illustration), simultaneously jumping up and forward with the right. While withdrawing the left leg close to the chest, front snap kick, this time with the right leg. As the second kick is completed, the body should be at its highest point. Withdraw the right leg and land in the original position, being sure to resume good posture and balance. Full use of the knee-snapping action in both kicks is necessary for the correct performance of this technique. At the beginning, a good way to practice is to kick first with the left leg, then without withdrawing it, to jump up and kick with the right leg, or vice versa.

Flying Side Kick (*yoko-tobi-geri*)

Like the flying front kick, this technique is most commonly used as a surprise attack, but it may also be used after dodging an opponent's attack, as a counterattack to the side of his neck.

From the forward stance, jump up with the left leg (in this illustration), simultaneously bringing the right knee close to the chest. Then, while pulling the left leg in close to the body, execute a side thrust kick (page 128) with the right. As the kick is completed, the body should be at its highest point. Withdraw the kicking leg and return to original position, being sure to resume correct posture and balance.

Note: In the flying kicks described on these two pages, it is extremely important to withdraw the leg close to the body immediately after kicking in order to maintain balance on landing, since it is at that point that you are most vulnerable.

Knee Kick (*hittsui-geri*)

This technique is particularly effective in close-in fighting. It may be performed straight upward to the front or in a circular motion from the side to the front. It is a strong technique for attacking opponent's abdomen, solar plexus, chest, ribs, or—after pulling him off balance—his face.

1. Front knee kick

Lift the knee and bend it sharply, then kick it up and forward. The back should be straight at the point of impact. The supporting leg should be bent slightly at the knee and ankle and held strongly. Illustrated on the right is the front knee kick being delivered to the opponent's face after pushing his head down.

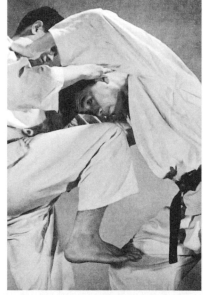

2. Roundhouse knee kick

Bend the knee sharply and lift it to the side; then, with a swivellike movement of the hips, swing the knee in a large circular motion to the target. Shown on the right is a roundhouse knee kick to the opponent's ribs, after closing in and blocking his attack.

BLOCKING TECHNIQUES

Besides attacking techniques, there are also a number of blocking techniques using the feet. One of the outstanding features of karate is that many attacking techniques can also be used for blocking; e.g., a punching or kicking attack can often be effectively blocked with a front or side kick. In the following pages, two of the most common blocking techniques using the feet are shown. Two important points which should be kept in mind are, first, that the blocking leg must be quickly withdrawn in order to prepare for the next technique; and secondly that secure balance must be maintained throughout the performance of the technique. Leg blocking techniques are especially valuable when for one reason or another the hands are not available for use.

Inside Snapping Block (*nami-ashi*)

This is a defensive technique against an attack to the groin and also to escape a stamping attack to the leg. In both cases it is very speedy.

The basic technique is best practiced from the straddle-leg stance. Since it is performed quickly, the body weight is not shifted. Its chief advantage lies in the fact that only the blocking leg is moved, leaving the rest of the body free to prepare for the next technique. Using the spring of the knee, kick the bottom of the foot upward in front of the body and immediately return it to original position. Force should be exerted from the hip muscles to give a "snap" to the upward movement.

Adaptation: This technique may be performed from the straddle-leg stance, diagonal straddle-leg stance, forward stance, and from a variety of freestyle stances.

Application: Here is an example of the inside snapping block being used against a front-kick attack to the groin. Note that the center of gravity of the man who is blocking does not shift.

Crescent-Kick Block
(*mikazuki-geri-uke*)

This is the crescent kick (page 135) used as a block. It is the most frequently used foot blocking technique. Special care must be taken to withdraw the leg rapidly after blocking.

There are many ways to shift to the offensive after blocking with the crescent-kick block. Illustrated here is one of the most common ones—the blocking leg is withdrawn to the chest and then immediately used in a side thrust kick, without lowering it to the ground.

13
Techniques in Combination

The possible combinations and sequences of techniques in karate are practically countless. For purposes of training, every type must be practiced so that the proper sequence of techniques called for in a given situation will be chosen more or less automatically. This includes shifting from a blocking technique to an attacking technique, from one attacking technique to the next attacking technique, from a hand technique to a foot technique, from a foot technique to a hand technique, etc.

Since the ultimate aim of karate is self-defense, blocking the opponent's attack and attacking for the purpose of destroying the ability of the opponent to attack are two sides of the same coin. The most common form of combination is blocking and almost simultaneously counterattacking with the hands or feet.

The ideal to be aimed at in karate is to accomplish one's purpose in the minimum number of movements, either by deterring the opponent from further attack by the use of one powerful block, or to counterattack strongly enough to make him unable to attack again. However, when one's own attack is blocked or not properly focused or when one is attacked by more than one opponent, a series of attacking techniques becomes necessary.

While blocking an attack it is obvious that one must assume the most advantageous position for applying the counterattack to follow, for breaking the opponent's balance, and for maintaining one's own balance. If the position turns out to be disadvantageous, one must change blocking hands and move into a better position. When subject to a continuing barrage of attacks, one must be able to continuously block them. Thus, training in sequential blocking is essential.

Even though they may be performed in combination or rapid sequence, it is important that each technique be focused individually. More so than in single techniques, in performing combination techniques the following points must be carefully borne in mind:

- Balance
- Muscular control
- Use of body dynamics
- Switch-over from one technique to the next
- Shifting body weight

The following pages give illustrations of each of these principles.

Balance

Special attention must be paid to maintaining good balance while performing techniques in combination, since movement from one technique to the next automatically creates the possibility of becoming unbalanced. Preservation of balance depends on properly executed techniques, correct posture, and strong stance.

Shown above is a combination sequence consisting of a reverse punch, a front kick, and a roundhouse kick. Note that the posture of the upper part of the body is properly maintained for each technique, and that it corresponds to the direction of execution of the techniques. The foot of the supporting leg is planted firmly on the ground, and the knee and ankle are tensed at points of impact. Balance may be lost in combinations like this by lifting the heel off the floor, leaning the body too far forward, exerting too much strength from the shoulders, and by not pulling the knee of the kicking leg close in to the chest before putting it down.

Shown below is a sequence combination of a crescent-kick block and a side thrust kick performed with the same leg. To preserve balance, the supporting leg must be in a strong stance and the upper part of the body kept as straight as possible.

Muscular Control

Since most karate techniques are focused at the point of impact, in performing a sequence of techniques the muscles must be tensed and relaxed with careful timing. If the muscles are held under tension after one technique is completed, smooth mobility into the next one is interfered with. This is why it is a basic principle in karate that the strength should be withdrawn from any technique immediately after it has been focused.

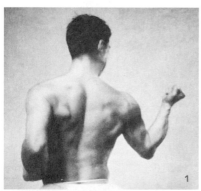

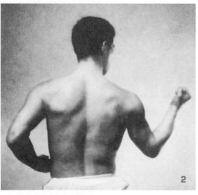

Illustrated above is a combination sequence of an outside forearm block, a sideward elbow strike, and a back-fist strike. Since these pictures don't clearly reveal the stages of muscular control, examine the photographs at left. The first shows the condition of the upper part of the body at the instant of focusing; the second, just before moving into the next technique.

Use of Body Dynamics

In performing a sequence of techniques, it is necessary to move smoothly and with a minimum of extraneous motion from the posture at the end of one technique into the next.

Within the limited range of this movement, the strength inherent in it must be applied to the second technique.

Shown above is a combination of a rising block and a reverse punch. The block is performed from a half-front-facing posture. In performing the reverse punch from this position, the rotational motion of the hips is used to add force to the punch.

The pictures below show an example of the straight punch and reverse punch being performed in sequence. In this case, rather subtle movements of the body are utilized—in relaxing the muscles following the focus of the right-hand straight punch, the left hip moves slightly backward as a sort of recoil; this slight hip movement is then reversed to perform the reverse punch, without actually pulling the hips back as in the basic reverse punch.

Shown below are the left side thrust kick and right roundhouse kick in sequence. Here the use of the swivel movement of the hips in shifting to the second kick is clearly visible.

Switch-over from One Technique to the Next

In executing a switch-over from one technique to the next, the change must be made with maximum economy of movement, smoothly, and with correct form.

Shown above is the execution of a spear-hand thrust from the knife-hand block position. In this sequence, the thrusting hand is moved from the guard position in front of the chest directly into the thrust without pulling it back to the normal starting position beside the hip.

Illustrated below is the rising block performed while taking a step forward after completing a reverse punch. This sequence requires that the hand be withdrawn slightly more than halfway toward the body and the block performed from there.

The above examples indicate a basic principle in switchover, namely, that in performing techniques in sequence the part of the body involved must enter the basic fixed course of the technique smoothly and by the quickest route.

Shown above is a side kick followed by a front kick with the opposite foot, but in the same direction. The point being emphasized here is that after completing the side kick and while moving into the front kick, the body must, without fail, face in the direction of the kick.

The pictures below show a front kick followed by a side kick with the opposite foot, but in the same direction. In performing the second kick in this case, the body must without fail face at right angles to the direction of the kick.

Summing up, in combination kicking the point to be emphasized is that the body must face in the proper direction with respect to the target before performing the second kick. Of course, this position must be assumed smoothly and not jerkily.

Shifting the Body Weight

Shifting the center of gravity of the body correctly is especially important in performing techniques in sequence. With proper timing, this shifting can add greatly to the strength of the technique. On the other hand, if the timing is off or the weight not shifted smoothly, not only is the technique weakened, but balance is jeopardized as well.

Shown on the right is a spear-hand thrust being performed while shifting from a back stance to a forward stance. In this case the body weight is shifted forward, adding to the force of the thrust.

Shown here is a reverse punch being performed from a downward block position in the forward stance. Neither stance nor position is changed. This is an example of a case where the center of gravity of the body does not change, although the twisting movement of the hips is used to add force to the punch.

Shown below are a front kick and a lunge punch being performed in sequence. Note that the body weight is shifted forward smoothly in conjunction with the ongoing techniques.

Examples of Common Combination Techniques

Combinations of blocking and attacking

- Downward block (fs) *—reverse punch (fs)
- Rising block (fs)—reverse punch (fs)
- Knife-hand block (fs)—spear-hand thrust (fs)
- Forearm block (fs)—reverse punch (fs)
- Forearm block (ss)—sideward elbow strike (ss)—back-fist strike
- Downward block (fs)—front kick
- Rising block (fs)—front kick
- Knife-hand block (bs)—front kick (with front foot)—spear-hand thrust (fs)
- Outside forearm block (fs)—roundhouse kick
- Inside forearm block (fs)—front kick—(st) reverse punch (fs)
- Crescent-kick block—side kick (same leg)

Combinations of attacking techniques

- Straight punch (fs)—back-fist strike (to the side) (fs)
- Lunge punch (fs)—(st) front kick
- Front kick—(st) lunge punch (fs)
- Reverse punch (fs)—front kick (with rear leg)—(st)roundhouse kick (with opposite leg)
- Front kick—(st) side kick (with other leg)—(st) reverse punch

Combinations of blocking techniques

- Downward block (fs)—rising block (either hand) (fs)
- Forearm block (fs)—rising block (either hand) (fs)
- Knife-hand block (fs)—inside forearm block (with opposite hand) (fs)
- Downward block (fs)—downward block (with opposite hand) (fs)
- Forearm block (fs)—forearm block (with opposite hand) (fs)

*(fs)=forward stance
 (bs)=back stance
 (ss)=straddle-leg stance
 (st)=stepping (actual change of position of body)

14
Formal Exercise

The so-called formal exercises, or forms (*kata*), consist of a systematically organized series of techniques performed in a set sequence. They include all the various hand techniques, foot techniques, body shifting, etc. used in kicking, punching, blocking, and so on. Before the modern system of sparring was developed, these formal exercises were the major form of karate practice.

Most of the formal exercises were created by famous karate masters, and into them are skillfully woven the various techniques of defense and attack. Most of them are based on the imagined existence of four or eight enemies. They provided the base from which present-day karate techniques developed, and are still the textbook of the art.

There are more than fifty formal exercises handed down from the past. Some are very old; others are of more recent origin. There are relatively simple ones, extremely complicated ones, those requiring agile movement, others depending on muscular or breath control. Modern students of karate are urged to master a variety of them, rather than concentrating on any one.

Advantages of Practicing Formal Exercises

For those who want to master the art of karate, rigorous practice of the formal exercises is strongly recommended. Some of their strong points are:

- They enable one to practice alone, no equipment is required, and any area big enough to move about in will suffice.
- Because they involve various kinds of movements, in every direction, they provide good all-around exercise and do not develop any one set of muscles at the expense of the others.
- Because they are based on the imagined existence of four or eight enemies attacking from several directions, they provide excellent practice in the adaptation of the various hand and foot techniques to various kinds of situations.
- Because of their short duration of only a few minutes, they are not too exhausting but at the same time provide a great deal of exercise, particularly after the techniques have been mastered so that each one can be strongly focused.

Schematic Diagram

The formal exercises are constructed in such a way that every movement—forward, backward, left, right, or diagonal—is performed along a fixed course, which may be represented in a schematic diagram. This makes the exercise easy to learn, and a mistaken movement is immediately apparent. Some formal exercises describe a straight line, others a T, an H, or more complicated figures. In all cases, however, the starting point and the finishing point coincide. This is the final test of whether the amount of stepping and the direction were correct throughout the exercise.

Hints on Mastering Formal Exercises

Besides consisting of the correct performance of a number of individual techniques, the formal exercise itself is an organic unit and must be mastered as if it were a single technique. Therefore, throughout the exercise attention must be paid to proper tensing and relaxing of the muscles of the body, extending and withdrawing the striking points of the body, speed and rhythm, etc. These are the "cautions" emphasized by karate masters in the early days of the art. Also important are correct posture, rhythmic expenditure of energy, correct facing of imagined enemies, etc.

A Representative Formal Exercise

Explained and illustrated on the following pages is the formal exercise known as Heian No. 4, which contains the most basic—and at the same time the most important—blocks, punches, strikes, kicks, body shifts, etc.

There are five so-called Heian formal exercises, which from the point of view of modern karate are the most basic and practical. They are usually the first to be learned by beginning students. Formerly called by the Chinese word Ping-an, probably after the name of the master who created them, they were changed to their present Japanized form by Gichin Funakoshi around 1920.

Among the five Heian exercises, the fourth has the most variation. It consists of twenty-seven movements, and after being learned takes about forty seconds to perform.

Schematic Diagram of Heian No. 4

The numbers refer to the sequence of movements, and the black dots correspond to the location of the body at the end of each successive movement.

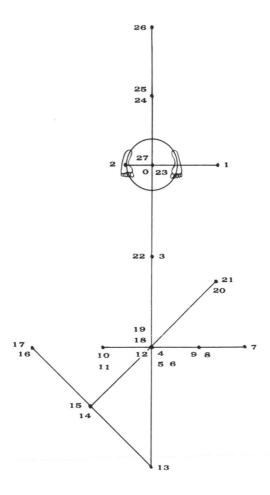

The following pages contain a movement-by-movement breakdown of this formal exercise. Just beneath the top row of photographs will be found in reduced size a portion of the schematic diagram shown above. Superimposed on each of these are illustrations of the feet, which show position and direction relative to the whole exercise and, in the case of intermediate movements, the direction and movement of the feet. The heavy arrows indicate the direction toward which the technique is performed. Each completed movement is indicated by a roman numeral above the respective photograph. The length of the arrow beside the roman numeral indicates the relative speed with which the next technique should be performed.

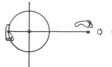

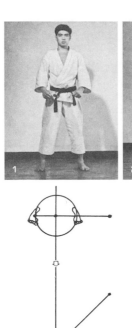

Heian No. 4 Form

1. Relaxed open-leg stance.
2. Move the left leg to the left and ū left back-hand up.
3. Assume back stance with weight on right leg; block an attack to the side of the face with a left back-hand block, forearm perpendicular to the ground; right hand in guard position in front of forehead.
4. Shifting weight to the left, repeat the same technique to the right.

After blocking a punching attack to the side of the head, move into forward stance and attack with a knife-hand strike to the neck; or from the back stance, attack with a front kick with the front leg.

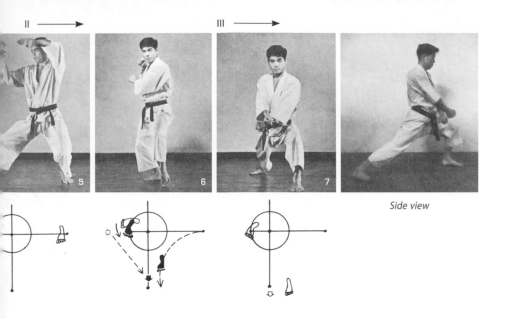

Side view

5. Back stance with weight on left leg; right back-hand block.
6. Move left leg to the front; clench fists and cross the left over the right.
7. Assume forward stance and thrust crossed fists diagonally downward in an X-block; keep back straight.

Move in and block the opponent's front-kick attack in its initial stages with a downward X-block.

Side view

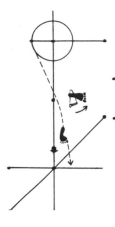

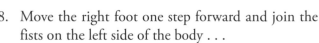

8. Move the right foot one step forward and join the fists on the left side of the body . . .

9. . . . Then assume back stance and execute an augmented right forearm block.

10. Lift the left foot to the knee of the right leg and join the fists on the right side of the body; left thigh parallel to the ground and right leg slightly bent.

After the opponent's kick is blocked, he attacks again with a punch to the abdomen. Block with an augmented forearm block, using the augmenting arm to help the blocking arm push down the attacker's arm. Shift to forward stance to throw the opponent off balance, and quickly change hands. Pressing the opponent's arm down, attack with a close punch to the jaw.

11. Execute a side snap kick with the left leg and a simultaneous sideward back-fist strike with the left hand; take care not to strike too high.
12. Withdraw the kicking leg, shifting weight in the direction of the kick.
13. Move into forward stance and place unclenched left hand in front of body as target.
14. Execute a forward strike with the right elbow, striking the left hand; be sure to keep the body low and fully utilize the swing of the hips.

Dodging the opponent's attack, counterattack with a side snap kick to the solar plexus and simultaneously a back-fist strike to the side of the face. Then grasp the opponent's lapels and attack the solar plexus with a sideward elbow strike.

15. Pull the left leg a half-step back toward the right leg, swing the body 180° to the right, and lift the right foot to the knee of the left leg (reverse of position in V).
16. Side snap-kick with the right foot, simultaneously executing a sideward back-fist strike.
17. Withdraw the kicking leg, shift weight in the direction of the kick, move into forward stance, and place the right hand out as a target.
18. Strike the right hand with the left elbow.

Side view

19. Block an attack from the left upward with right knife-hand, and simultaneously block downward with left knife-hand.
20. Twist the upper part of the body 180° to the left; swing the right hand widely to the outside, simultaneously raising the left hand in front of the face.
21. Execute an outside knife-hand strike to the neck and block upward with left knife-hand.

Simultaneously block a kicking attack from the left downward with a knife-hand and block a punching attack upward. Upward-block the next attack and counterattack with a knife-hand strike to the neck.

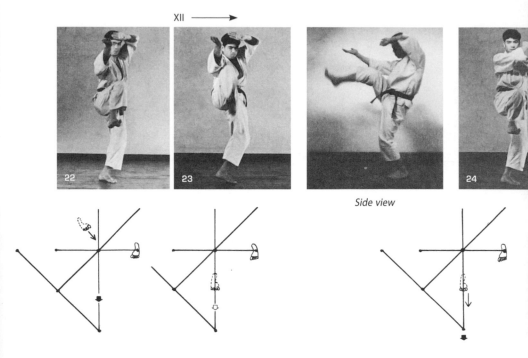

Side view

22. Without changing position of hands or upper part of body, shift weight forward and begin front kick.
23. Keeping the hands in place, front snap kick as high as possible, taking care not to raise the heel of the supporting leg.
24. Follow through the kick by shifting weight forward, withdrawing the leg sharply to the chest; bring the right fist to the left ear, simultaneously extending the left hand, palm downward.

After focusing the knife-hand strike, attack again with a front kick to the opponent's solar plexus. As he attempts a punching attack, press his hand down, move in close, and counterattack with a downward backfist strike to his solar plexus.

Side view

25. Place the right foot down forward and bring the left foot quickly to the right of the right heel, with toes facing the right heel and the left heel off the ground; at the same time, execute a downward back-fist strike with the right hand, pulling the left sharply back to the hip; to maintain balance, keep posture low.

26. With the right foot as the fulcrum, swing 225° to the left, stepping forward with the left foot; keep right knee bent; cross fists in front of chest, left fist in front.

(Note that, although at this point you are facing in the opposite direction from the starting position, the orientation of the diagram is not reversed.)

27. From back stance, execute a wedge block.

As the opponent approaches you from behind, swing completely around to face him from a back stance. As he attempts to grasp your lapels, execute a strong wedge block.

28. Keeping the hands in the same position, shift weight forward and front snap kick with the right foot, fully utilizing the snap of the knee.
29. With hands still in the same position, withdraw the leg and continue to shift your weight forward.
30. As the kicking foot touches the ground, assume a forward stance and lunge punch to the midsection; do not pull the arm back to standard position before punching.
31. From the same position, quickly reverse hands and execute a reverse punch with the left hand.

After wedge-blocking the opponent's attack, shift weight forward and attack with a front snap kick with the rear foot. Placing the kicking foot down forward, assume forward stance and deliver a lunge punch, then a reverse punch. (Note: One of the advantages of moving into a back stance in conjunction with the wedge block is that it facilitates pulling the opponent off balance before kicking.)

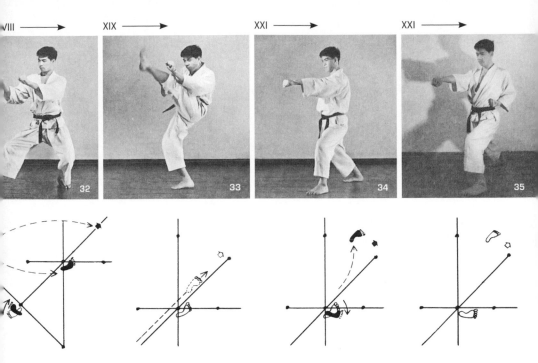

32. Pivot on the left foot 90° to the right, moving the right foot in an inside arc; assume back stance and execute a wedge block; in rotating do not straighten the legs.
33. Snap kick forward with the rear foot as in XV.
34. Assume forward stance and execute a straight punch as in XVI.
35. Without changing position, execute a reverse punch as in XVII.

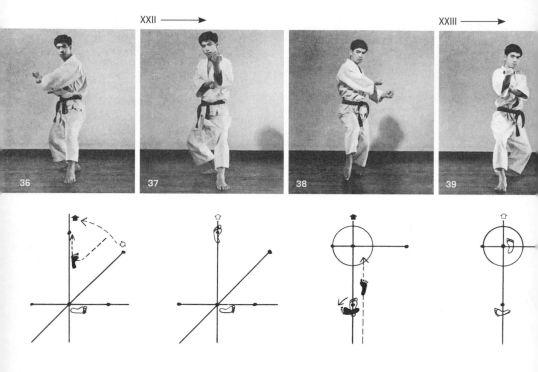

36. With the right foot stationary, swing the left leg in an inside arc 45° to the left; swing both fists back near the right shoulder.
37. Assume back stance and execute a left augmented forearm block; at this point you should be facing exactly the opposite direction from the starting position.
38. Step forward with the right foot, and swing fists near the left shoulder.
39. Assume back stance and execute a right augmented forearm block.

As the opponent makes a punching attack from the left, block with an augmented forearm block. As explained in a previous section, this position affords an opportunity to counterattack with the front leg or the blocking arm. Shown below is another application, where the blocking arm of the first augmented forearm block is used to hold the opponent's arm while a second inside forearm block is performed against the same arm in a scissors-like motion, cracking his elbow joint.

40   41   42

side view

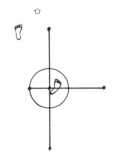

40. Step forward with the left foot, and from back stance execute a left augmented forearm block. While performing the movements in XXII, XXIII, and XXIV, keep the legs bent so that the head does not bob up and down.
41. Move the left leg half a step to the left so that forward stance is assumed; unclench the hands and start thrusting them outward and upward.
42. Fully extend arms and hands at the level of the face, as if to grasp the back of the opponent's head.

Close in on the opponent by moving into forward stance, extend arms and hands, grasp the back of the opponent's head and pull it down, at the same time lifting the knee up to strike his face.

Side view　　*Back view*

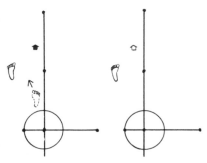  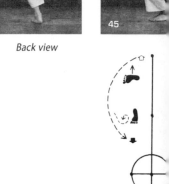

43. Bend and raise the right knee, simultaneously clenching the fists and pulling them forcibly down toward the knee.
44. Complete the movement of the hands, simultaneously executing a knee kick at stomach level.
45. Place the right foot down one step forward, and pivoting on the left foot swing 180° counterclockwise; simultaneously raise the left hand next to the right ear and the right hand under the armpit.

As the opponent approaches to attack from the rear, quickly swing around and execute a knife-hand block.

Side view

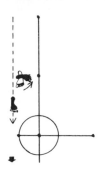

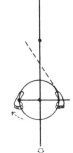

46. Assume back stance and execute a left knife-hand block; to maintain balance in swinging around, keep the weight low.
47. Step forward with the rear foot; place the right hand next to the left ear and the left hand under the right armpit.
48. Assume back stance and execute a right knife-hand block.
49. Bring the left foot one step diagonally forward and resume open-leg stance; you should now be in the same position as at the beginning of the exercise.

After blocking, move into forward stance and attack with a spear-hand thrust to the solar plexus, then step forward into back stance and attack again with a knife-hand strike to the neck, all the while grasping the opponent's arm. Of course, the two consecutive knife-hand blocks of the exercise may also be viewed simply as blocks.

15
Sparring

As the word suggests, sparring (*kumite*) in karate is a method of practicing the various techniques while facing an actual opponent. In its early days, the main forms of karate practice were the formal exercises, and except for occasional tests of strength (*kake-dameshi*) of the various punches, kicks, and blocks, there was no sparring as such.

In the 1920s, under the leadership of Gichin Funakoshi, a system of elementary sparring was devised. This was gradually developed and refined into the present-day freestyle sparring, which can be performed as a competitive match.

Because karate in its early days was used in fighting actual armed enemies and was itself perfected into a dangerous weapon, it wasn't until it became associated with the other Japanese martial arts that the concept of focusing the techniques just short of contact with the opponent was developed, making sparring possible. Mutual trust between opponents, which is said to be an important feature of the "morality" of Japanese martial arts, is expressed in the rules of freestyle sparring, where any attack which actually strikes a vital point of the opponent is forbidden.

Besides giving the student practice in hand techniques, foot techniques, and body shifting, sparring also trains him in distancing (i.e., keeping the

proper distance between oneself and one's opponent necessary for the execution of the technique one has chosen), timing, and responding. Strategy is called for, as well as courage and composure.

There are two types of sparring: one in which the mode of attack is determined and agreed upon in advance; and the other freestyle, in which nothing is predetermined. Within the former are basic sparring and semi-free sparring.

Basic Sparring (*kihon kumite*)

In basic sparring, the two participants face each other from a fixed distance and take turns attacking and defending. In every case, the mode of attack and target are predetermined. It could appropriately be called a formal exercise in sparring. The purpose of basic sparring is to train beginners in the principles of applying techniques. The examples given in this section are only the most representative. By referring to the techniques explained in previous sections, and applying them in similar ways, the reader will be able to devise many other combinations worth practicing.

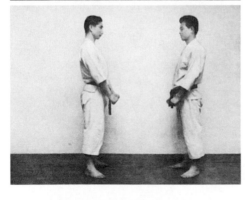

Standard Procedure in Basic Sparring

1. Players face each other in open-leg stance at a distance that will enable the attacker to take one step forward and just make contact with his opponent.

2. The attacker assumes the position most appropriate for the predetermined mode of attack. In most cases, this consists of the forward stance, as shown in the illustration. The right foot is to the rear for a right-handed attack and the left foot to the rear for a left-handed attack. The attacking hand is placed on the hip and the opposite hand extended outward in a downward-blocking position. The defender remains in an open-leg stance. Both players should avoid being overly tense at this point.

3. The attacker attacks as predetermined; the defender blocks or dodges and counterattacks.

4. After the counterattack is completed, both parties withdraw smoothly to the starting position. Whether defending or attacking, the eyes should be focused steadily on the opponent's eyes. This may seem unnecessary in basic sparring, but it is a good idea to avoid the habit of carelessness in the face of an imminent attack, which will be the case when the student advances to freestyle sparring.

Representative Examples

Stepping back, blocking a punching attack, and then counterattacking

1. Attacker assumes forward stance, with one hand in downward-blocking position, then steps forward and delivers lunge punch. The defender moves one step back, blocks with a rising block, and counterattacks with a reverse punch to the solar plexus. In this as well as in the other examples which follow, as proficiency is developed, the length of time between blocking and counterattacking should gradually be shortened. It is also important to practice grabbing, pulling, or pushing the opponent's attacking arm to throw him off balance. In these defenses involving stepping back, be sure that the rear leg assumes a firm stance and that the body does not lean backward. The chief advantage of stepping-back defenses is that they allow the defender to control the distance between himself and his opponent.

2. As the defender is attacked with a punching attack to the solar plexus, he steps back and blocks with an outside forearm block, then counterattacks with a roundhouse kick to the temple.

3. As he is attacked with a punching attack to the face, the defender steps back and blocks with an upward X-block, then counterattacks with a front kick to the jaw.

Stepping in, blocking a punching attack, and then counterattacking

1. A: Delivers a lunge-punch attack to the face.

   D: Timing his movements to those of the attacker, steps in with his right foot next to the attacker's right foot, assumes straddle-leg stance and blocks with an outside forearm block, then counterattacks with a sideward elbow strike to the solar plexus. In these defensive movements involving stepping in, timing and a good strong stance are especially important. The outstanding advantage of this kind of defense is that it enables the defender to stop the attack before it is fully focused, making it easy to throw the attacker off balance.

Note: In the following sequences "A" refers to the attacker and "D" refers to the defender.

2. A: Delivers a lunge punch attack to the face.
   D: Steps into forward stance, blocks with a rising block, then simultaneously grasping opponent's hand and pulling him off balance, counterattacks with a forward elbow strike. In this instance it is important to assume a relatively low forward stance in order to block the opponent's punch from well below.

3. A: Delivers a lunge punch to the solar plexus.
   D: Steps in and blocks with a downward block, then counterattacks with a front knee kick to the solar plexus.

4. A: Delivers a lunge punch to the solar plexus.
   D: Steps into forward stance and blocks from the inside with an augmented forearm block, then with the augmenting arm delivers a close punch to the jaw.

Simultaneously blocking and shifting sideways to the inside of a punching attack, and then counterattacking

1. A: Delivers a left lunge punch to the solar plexus.

   D: Timing his movements to those of the opponent, he shifts to the left; inside of attacking assumes back stance and blocks with a knife-hand block. Then he counterattacks with a front kick to the solar plexus with the forward leg, maintaining the back-stance angle of rear leg. In all cases involving shifting to the inside, timing is especially important. If the shift is made too soon, the attacker still has time to change the direction of his attack; if the shift is delayed, there won't be enough time to shift before blocking. In defensive maneuvers involving shifting to the inside, the counterattack must be delivered quickly, for the opponent is still in a good position to renew the attack. The advantages of this type of defense are that a strong attack can be successfully blocked with a minimum of strength and opponent's vulnerable points are fully exposed.

2. A: Delivers a lunge punch to the face.
   D: Shifts sideways inside of the attack and blocks with extended knife-hand block (arm fully extended, wrist bent upward), then counterattacks with a reverse punch to the solar plexus.

3. A: Delivers a lunge punch to the solar plexus.
   D: Shifts sideways inside of the attack, downward blocks from straddle-leg stance, then counterattacks with a side kick to the face or the solar plexus. (As a rule, the snap kick is used when close in, and the thrust kick when farther away.)

Simultaneously blocking and shifting to the outside of a punching attack, and then counterattacking

1. A: Delivers a left lunge punch to the face.
   D: Shifting to the right outside of the attack, blocks with a knife-hand block from cat stance, then counterattacks with a front kick to the armpit. Just as in shifting to the inside, in shifting to the outside timing is important. The advantages of this defensive technique are that the opponent is poorly situated to attack again and little strength is required to block a strong attack. Of course, if the shift is made too far to the outside, the opponent will be able to change position and renew his attack.

2. A: Delivers a lunge punch to the solar plexus.
   D: Shifting to the outside, blocks from a straddle-leg stance with a downward block, then counterattacks with a side kick to the armpit.

3. A: Delivers a lunge punch to the solar plexus.
   D: Shifting to the outside, blocks from a forward stance with an extended knife-hand block, then counterattacks with a roundhouse kick to the ribs.

Simultaneously blocking a punching attack and counterattacking

These defensive techniques are very effective, but to a certain extent more difficult to perform than those shown in the previous pages. The blocks are performed in the same basic manner as has been explained earlier, the only difference being that the counterattacks are delivered simultaneously. There is a natural tendency for either the block or the counterattack to be weak; therefore, it is essential to choose a block and a counterattack each of which will augment the force of the other.

1. A: Delivers a lunge punch to the face.
   D: Steps in, and simultaneously blocks with a rising knife-hand block and counterattacks with an outside knife-hand strike to the side of the neck.

2. A: Delivers lunge punch to the solar plexus.
   D: Steps back, and simultaneously downward blocks and counterattacks with reverse punch.
3. A: Delivers lunge punch to the solar plexus.
   D: Steps back about half a step, and simultaneously downward blocks and counterattacks with front kick to the groin, using the foot that stepped back. The step back is necessary to create the proper distance from the opponent for a front kick.

Simultaneously shifting and counterattacking

1. A: Delivers a right lunge punch to the face.
   D: Shifts to the left, avoiding the blow, and counterattacks with a back-fist strike to the ribs from straddle-leg stance. In defensive techniques where the opponent's attack is dodged rather than blocked, speed, smoothness, and timing are essential. The counterattack must be commenced while shifting.

2. A: Delivers a lunge punch to the solar plexus.
   D: Dodges to the inside of the attack and counterattacks with a front kick to the chin. Be sure to lift the kicking foot to the knee of the upporting leg before kicking.

3. A: Delivers a lunge punch to the solar plexus.
   D: Shifts outside of the attack, and from forward stance, counterattacks with an outside ridgehand strike to the temple.

Anticipating a punching attack and counterattacking

1. A: Starts a right lunge punch to the solar plexus.
   D: As opponent starts to attack, immediately counterattacks with a lunge punch to the face. The performance of this and similar techniques requires fast thinking in order to attack the opponent at the instant when and at the place where he is most vulnerable. The obvious advantage of this kind of defensive technique is that it produces a strong counterattack, since the movement of the opponent into the blow enhances its power. It requires superior timing, instant finding of an opening, rapid movement, and courage.

2. A: Starts a lunge punch to the face.
   D: As the opponent starts to attack, counterattacks with a side thrust kick to the solar plexus (above); or outside stamp-kicks the knee of the opponent's front leg, then delivers a roundhouse kick to the ribs (below). In either case, in spite of the necessity for speed, the kicking foot must be raised to the knee of the supporting leg before kicking.

Blocking a kicking attack and counterattacking

Since kicking attacks are stronger than punches, they must be strongly blocked or securely dodged. If possible, advantage should be taken of the fact that the opponent momentarily has only one foot on the ground.

A: Delivers a left side thrust kick to the solar plexus.

D: Shifts to the right (outside) and downward blocks from straddle-leg stance, then counterattacks with a front kick to the groin.

A: Delivers a roundhouse kick to the face.

D: Steps back, and from forward stance blocks with an inside forearm block, then counterattacks with a reverse punch to the solar plexus. In this case, the block is focused further to the outside than usual.

A: Delivers a front kick to the solar plexus.

D: Steps back to the inside of the attack and downward blocks from forward stance; then, throwing the opponent off balance with the blocking arm, counterattacks to the face with a reverse punch.

Semi-Free One-Blow Sparring (*jiyū-ippon kumite*)

As in basic sparring, in this practice technique the mode of attack and the vital point to be attacked are prearranged. However, both attacker and defender assume relaxed ready positions and move about. The attacker must find an opening and create the proper distance from his opponent before attacking. The defender must watch for the attack and be ready to defend himself. As soon as the attack comes he must block or dodge then counterattack. This type of sparring approaches the more advanced freestyle sparring, although the same techniques are used as in basic sparring. The student should apply dynamically the examples given in basic sparring. This is a midway step between basic and

freestyle sparring. It gives excellent training in distancing, finding an opening, and correct and speedy use of techniques in action. Both attacker and defender must attempt to distance properly, one for the purpose of attacking and the other for the purpose of defending.

After the student has acquired a degree of proficiency in this type of sparring, a more advanced variation is to predetermine the attacker and defender, but to attack at any point and in any way desired.

The ready position in semi-free one-blow sparring consists of any which is appropriate for respectively attacking or defending. Any position in which the muscles are under tension is not proper, since instantaneous movement will be hampered. A natural, relaxed stance is the most effective. More movement than is necessary should be avoided, since it jeopardizes balance. In closing up a gap between himself and his opponent, the attacker should advance quickly with a sliding step. When he is too close in for a lunge punch he should pull his front leg back next to the rear leg and then step forward with the rear leg. In most cases, the attack in semi-free sparring takes the form of a lunge punch.

Freestyle Sparring (*jiyū-kumite*)

This is a completely free form of sparring in which neither the form of attack nor the attacker is prearranged. It resembles sparring in boxing, except that the attacks are pulled just short of contact with the target. The rules of freestyle sparring strictly prohibit any needless action which is liable to injure the opponent, such as stamping his instep more strongly than is necessary, or striking with great force an arm which is not attacking.

Obviously, there is danger of serious injury if one of the participants actually strikes one of his opponent's vital points with a focused attack. However, one of the tests of proficiency in karate is the ability to focus even the strongest technique just short of contact with the target, so this danger is minimized.

Because it contains elements of both competition and uncertainty and can be played in earnest, freestyle sparring has steadily gained in popularity among karate enthusiasts in Japan. However, for beginners, besides being dangerous, it actually impedes their acquiring skill. It has been found that the best order of training is first of all practice in essential basic techniques, with emphasis on proper focusing, then basic sparring, one-blow semi-free sparring, and finally freestyle sparring.

The on-guard position in freestyle sparring is one of watchful, though relaxed, preparedness. The actual sparring consists of a free exchange of blows, blocks, and counterattacks, until one of the players gets in a focused attack at a vital point of his opponent. Participation in freestyle sparring requires expert use of hand and foot techniques, blocking, shifting, distancing, timing, responding, courage, composure, tactics—in other words, all aspects of advanced karate.

Tactics

When the opponent in freestyle sparring is securely on his guard, it is very difficult to get in a focused attack. It is only when there is an opening in his defenses that a successful attack can be made. Tactics in karate thus consists of finding or creating such an opening and taking best advantage of it.

The following chart shows the breakdown of openings in karate:

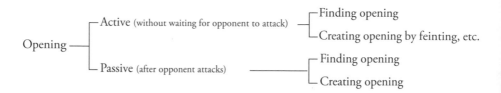

Opening
— Active (without waiting for opponent to attack)
— Finding opening
— Creating opening by feinting, etc.
— Passive (after opponent attacks)
— Finding opening
— Creating opening

Finding an opening in the opponent's defenses depends on training and experience and can hardly be explained here. The best way to take advantage of an opening once found or created depends on the proper application of the various techniques explained previously. The following pages contain examples of creating openings, both actively and passively.

Actively creating an opening

This may be accomplished by putting the opponent off guard psychologically, such as by pretending to relax or by shouting. Also effective is the judicious use of actual techniques, such as attacking or feinting an attack in one direction, thereby creating an opening elsewhere, or weakening the opponent's defenses by attacking in the same direction continuously, or throwing him off balance by attacking his leg, and so on. Here are a few representative examples.

Side thrust kick to the opponent's knee, drawing his attention there and throwing him off balance. This creates an opening at his face, which is then attacked with a roundhouse kick.

Thrust the heel of the palm toward the opponent's face, creating an opening at his midsection, which is then attacked with a lunge punch.

Crouch low as if preparing to attack the opponent's midsection; then deliver a roundhouse kick to the neck.

Passively creating an opening

This consists of enticing the opponent to attack by showing him an apparent opening and then taking advantage of the opening thus created in *his* defenses. As in the previous case, this is accomplished either by psychological means or by careful use of actual techniques.

By lowering your guard from the face and acting as if to attack to the midsection, lead the opponent to make an attack to the face, exposing his armpit, which is then attacked with a side kick.

Feinting an attack to the opponent's face will lead him to attempt an attack to your midsection, which is momentarily exposed. This creates an opening to his head, which is then attacked with a roundhouse kick to the temple.

Freestyle Sparring as a Sport

With the development of freestyle sparring, it became possible to conduct actual karate matches. The success of this kind of competition depends on highly trained techniques and an attitude of self-control on the part of both participants.

Contest rules for freestyle sparring have been laid down by the Japan Karate Association. Given below are selected paragraphs from the official rules embodying the most important points:

1. Karate contests shall be held within an area eight meters (about eight yards) square, marked off with a white or other easily visible border. The surface should be of a smooth, flat material such as polished wood or canvas-covered mats.
4. A single match shall last for either two or three minutes, according to the previous decision of the judges.
5. When no decision as to winner or loser is reached during the stipulated period, a one-minute rest period will be assigned, after which the match will be resumed for two minutes, followed by further one-minute rest periods and two-minute bouts until a decision is reached or the judges call a tie.

6. Judges
   a. One arbitrator shall view the match from such a vantage point that he can clearly see the entire contest area.
   b. One referee shall move freely about within the contest area.
   c. Four judges shall be posted at the four outside corners of the contest area.
7. Other officials
   a. Two or three timekeepers shall be seated at an appropriate and convenient location outside the contest area.
   b. Two or three starters shall likewise be posted at an appropriate location outside the contest area.
   c. Two or three recorders shall be posted similarly.
9. The first type is a one-blow match, in which the contestant who gets in the first "killing" blow wins.
10. The second type is a three-blow match, in which the contestant who gets in two "killing" blows out of three wins.
11. The third type of contest is a decision match, in which the winner is determined on the basis of points allotted by the judges.
12. In every case, the type of match to be performed shall be determined by the judges and communicated beforehand to the participants.
20. When neither contestant has succeeded in getting in a "killing" blow, the winner shall be determined by the decision of the judges. When one of the contestants is injured, likewise the winner shall be determined by the decision of the judges.
21. If one of the contestants commits a foul, he is automatically declared the loser.
22. When, for one reason or another, one of the contestants is disqualified, the other shall be declared the winner.
23. The contestant who forfeits before or during a match shall be declared the loser.
24. When an injury occurs during the contest and it cannot be continued, the decision of the judges shall be made on the following grounds:
   a. When the injured party is responsible for the injury, the other party wins.
   b. When the injury is caused by the other party, the injured party wins.
   c. When the responsibility for the injury cannot be determined, the judges shall declare a tie.
26. A completed, effective punch, strike, or kick strongly focused on one of the vital points listed in para. 28 below shall be recognized as a "killing" blow under the following conditions:
   a. Correct form

b. Correct attitude

c. Correct distance

27. A less than fully focused blow shall be recognized as a "killing" blow in the following cases:

a. When the opponent moves into the blow

b. When the opponent's balance is broken by a sequence of consecutive attacks

c. When the blow is delivered after throwing the opponent

28. The following vital points only are recognized targets for a "killing" blow:

a. Face

b. Neck

c. Midsection

29. The following criteria are established for allotting points:

a. Effective blow less than a "killing" blow—3 points

b. Commendable attitude—1 point

c. Good tactics—1 point

d. Skillful or strong techniques—1 point

e. Fighting spirit—1 point

f. When a contestant is reprimanded by the referee—3 points to opponent

g. Stepping outside contest area—1 point to opponent

h. Other factors determined by the judges

30. The following are strictly prohibited:

a. Actually hitting opponent's vital points with a punch, strike, or kick

b. Attempting to attack opponent's eyes with a spear-hand thrust

c. Biting or clawing

d. Holding or clinching unnecessarily

e. Performing dangerous throwing techniques or other acts liable to cause injury to opponent

f. Turning one's back to the opponent

g. Avoiding actual sparring contact with the opponent by stalling until the gong sounds

h. Swearing at the opponent, attempting to make him mad, or otherwise showing disrespect

32. The contestant shall be immediately disqualified in the following cases:

a. When he ignores the instructions of the referee

b. When he loses his temper to the point of endangering his opponent

c. Other unsportsmanlike behavior

16
Throwing Techniques

Throwing in karate is not an end in itself but a means to create an opening in the opponent's defenses, enabling one to get in a focused attack. This is usually accomplished by first making an ordinary attack and then deftly taking advantage of the force of the opponent's block to throw him, finally making a fully focused attack. In principle, karate throwing techniques do not vary from those used in judo or other grappling sports. What distinguishes them is that they are used in conjunction with and take advantage of the force of other attacking or blocking techniques.

Examples of Karate Throwing Techniques

Simultaneously block a punching attack to the face with a rising block and attack the opponent's jaw with a focused palm-heel strike. Then, utilizing the forward momentum of the opponent's body, grasp his wrist with the blocking hand, push against his jaw with the other, and pivoting on the front foot, swing around and back, lowering the knee to the ground and throwing the opponent down. Deliver the final attack with an elbow strike to the solar plexus. The main point to remember in executing this throw is to bring your body in close to that of the opponent.

Simultaneously block a punching attack to the face with a rising block and attack the opponent's groin with a palm-heel strike. Then, utilizing the momentum of the opponent's body, grasp his arm with the blocking hand, lift up between his legs with the other arm, and, twisting your hips around, swing him over your shoulders to the ground. Finally, attack his chest with an elbow strike. Be sure to place the shoulder of the arm thrust between the opponent's legs into his solar plexus.

Ducking a roundhouse kick to the face by dropping down on one knee, side thrust kick the opponent's supporting leg at the knee joint. As he falls to the ground, deliver a front stamping kick to the ribs.

 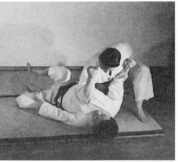

Strongly scoop-block the leg of the opponent as he attacks with a front kick, simultaneously moving in close to his supporting leg and throwing him to the ground. Finally, attack with a front kick to his ribs.

PART 3
Karate as Self-Defense

17
Defense
against Holding

A person well trained in the use of karate techniques can successfully defend himself against an adversary who attempts to hold, hug, or twist his arm or arms backward. Depending on the situation, he may escape and then counterattack or

counterattack first and then escape. In either case he must effectively utilize those parts of his body which can still be moved and take maximum advantage of the strength of his opponent or opponents. One of the chief advantages of karate in self-defense is that even if the upper part of the body is completely immobilized, the feet and legs can still be used to advantage. In spite of this, however, a good principle to remember is that every effort should be made to escape and/or counterattack before the opponent has had a chance to get in a hold, and to break a hold, once made, as quickly as possible.

Examples of Defense against Holding

A. When one hand is held by both of the opponent's hands.
Make a tight fist of the hand being held, place the free hand over it, and moving in with the elbow, pull the held hand back toward the body, simultaneously striking the opponent in the solar plexus with the elbow.

B. When both hands are held.
Take one step backward, pull hands sideward and downward as in the downward block, and kick the opponent in the groin or solar plexus with a front kick. It is possible to deliver the kick as soon as the hands are grabbed, but stepping back and pulling the opponent off balance makes it more effective. Also, it is much easier to spread the hands apart if they are first thrust together and then suddenly and forcibly pulled apart.

C. When an opponent grasps the lapels and attempts an attack to the face.
Block the punch with a strong outside forearm block and immediately attack opponent's solar plexus with an elbow strike. In the event that the opponent's arm grasping the lapels is too high to permit an effective outside block, block with the opposite arm, using an inside forearm block or hooking block, and counterattack with an elbow strike or close punch.

D. When an opponent grasps the lapels with both hands.
Insert both fists up between the opponent's hands, step quickly back into back stance, simultaneously wedge-blocking and breaking the opponent's balance; then pull the opponent's arms toward you and deliver a front kick to the solar plexus.

E. When an opponent attempts a bear hug from behind.

Step sideways and lower the body into straddle-leg stance, simultaneously raising both elbows; then counterattack with a roundhouse punch to the face and simultaneously an elbow strike to the solar plexus.

When the hold is too far down for the above technique to work, either back snap kick to the groin (left) or back stamp kick to the instep (right).

F. When held in a full nelson.

Thrust pelvis forward, reach back and attack the opponent's temples with a fore-knuckle-fist punch, then thrust the buttocks back to strike opponent in the groin, simultaneously swinging the arms down to attack his ribs with a second fore-knuckle-fist punch. Finally, if a further counterattack is called for, hold the opponent's hands tightly between the elbows and the body, move into forward stance, twist the hips and throw opponent to the ground, and then deliver the final punch.

G. When an opponent uses both hands to pull and twist the hand from behind.

Swing the foot opposite the hand being held around near the opponent and attack his face with a back-fist strike with the free hand. When the hand is being twisted, remember always to rotate the body in the direction that will ease the pressure on the wrist.

H. When opponent pulls your hand backward and pushes your shoulder forward.

Attack his solar plexus with a back thrust kick.

I. When two opponents pull both hands backward and hold your shoulders.

As shown in the previous example, attack one opponent with a back thrust kick. Then withdraw the leg, assume straddle-leg stance, and attack the other opponent with an elbow strike to the ribs. Make sure you don't lose your balance in executing this maneuver.

J. When two opponents pull hands sideward
Attack in rapid succession first one opponent and then the other with side snap kicks to the armpits. If the opponents are too far away for this technique to work, double-step sideways and deliver a side kick or a side thrust kick to the solar plexus.

K. When two opponents pull hands downward to the sides
Since it is impossible to kick sideways from this position, in one smooth movement lift leg as in crescent-kick block on top of (or between) one of the opponent's hands and then side thrust kick to his solar plexus. Then swing around and with same leg deliver a front kick to the other opponent's solar plexus.

L. When one opponent holds hands from behind and another opponent approaches to attack.

Block attacker's punch with crescent-kick block and with same leg quickly side thrust kick to his solar plexus. Then with same leg attack the other opponent with a back snap kick to the groin.

18
Defense from a Floor-Sitting Position

Even though the body is considerably immobilized when sitting on the floor Oriental-style, with practice it is possible to block an attack from this position.

Examples of Defense from a Floor-Sitting Position

A. When an opponent attempts to grab both hands.
Pull hands forcibly apart to the sides and simultaneously rise up on one knee and knee-kick to the opponent's solar plexus.

B. When an opponent threatens a punching attack.
Block with a rising block, grasp the attacking arm to pull the opponent off balance, and counterattack with a punch to the solar plexus. If possible, it is more effective to rise up on one knee in executing this technique.

C. When an opponent makes a kicking attack.
To dodge a front kick, lean your body to the side and counterattack with a side thrust kick to the groin.

When an opponent attacks with a roundhouse kick, fall diagonally to the front and counterattack with a roundhouse kick to the groin.

D. When an opponent makes a punching attack from the side.
Fall to the side to dodge the punch and counterattack with a side thrust kick to the armpit.

E. When an opponent attempts to attack with a roundhouse kick from the side.
Simultaneously pull the opponent's ankle with one hand and push his knee with the other, throwing him to the ground; then counterattack with an elbow strike to the solar plexus. In executing this technique it is necessary to move in close to the opponent very quickly.

F. When an opponent approaches to attack from the rear.

In the case of a punching attack, fall forward to dodge the blow and back thrust kick to the armpit (or solar plexus).

In the case of a kicking attack, fall diagonally forward to dodge the blow and side thrust kick to the groin.

G. When an opponent approaches from behind to make a choking attack.

Attack both temples with a fore-knuckle-fist punch, then grasp the opponent's lapels, lean forward, and throw him over your head; deliver the final counterattack with an elbow strike to the face.

19
Defense from a Chair-Sitting Position

When sitting in a chair, the body's center of gravity is located near the chair, and the lower part of the body is somewhat immobilized, but with practice, karate techniques can be effectively applied to thwart an attack from this position.

Examples of Defense from a Chair-Sitting Position

A. When an opponent sitting opposite rises to make a punching attack.

Block with an upward X-block; then pull the attacking hand down, simultaneously attacking the opponent's jaw with a front snap kick.

B. When a standing opponent attacks from the front

In the case of a punching attack, grasp the seat of the chair with both hands for balance; before the opponent can complete his attack, counterattack with a front thrust kick to the solar plexus.

When the attack takes the form of a front kick, quickly rise from the chair to the side to dodge the kick and counterattack with a side thrust kick to the ribs.

C. When an opponent sitting beside you suddenly attacks.

Block the punching attack to the face with an outside forearm block and immediately counterattack with an elbow strike to the solar plexus.

D. When an opponent standing to the side makes a punching attack.

Dodge sideways and counterattack with a side thrust kick to the ribs. Note that the defender places his hand on the floor for balance.

E. When an opponent standing to the side attacks with a side kick.

Dodge to the side and side thrust kick to the knee joint; then with the opposite foot deliver a roundhouse kick to the solar plexus.

F. When an opponent approaches from behind to make a punching attack.

Move one foot to the side toward the opponent and block the attack with an inside forearm block; then counterattack with a roundhouse kick to the face.

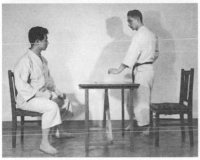

G. When an opponent sitting across a table stands up to attack.

Block the attack with an inside forearm block; then, passing the leg over the table, roundhouse kick to the opponent's neck.

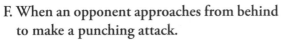

20
Defense against a Knife Attack

The techniques used to thwart or dodge an attack by an opponent armed with a knife and then to counterattack are basically the same as those used in sparring. However, special care must be taken to avoid being cut with the knife, and in actual application it's a good idea to make use of a piece of clothing, a shoe, or the like. There is a tendency to dodge too far from an armed attacker, making the counterattack difficult and giving the opponent a chance to attack again. Be sure to guard against this tendency.

Examples of Defense against a Knife Attack

A. When an opponent attempts a stabbing attack to the face.

Block the attacking arm with an extended knife-hand block and simultaneously side snap kick to the armpit (or, if there is sufficient distance, side thrust kick). Then lower the foot, grasp the attacking arm, pull the opponent off balance, and roundhouse kick to the temple. In this maneuver, for safety's sake it's a good idea to lean as far away as possible from the knife while blocking and making the first kick.

B. When an opponent attempts a stabbing attack to the stomach.

With careful timing, fall diagonally forward to the ground and roundhouse kick to the groin. It is necessary to slide into a position near the opponent's leg for this maneuver to be successful. After kicking the groin, it is possible to side thrust kick the opponent's knee joint with the same leg, throwing him to the ground, and then complete the counterattack.

C. When an opponent attempts a stabbing attack to the top of the head.

Step toward the opponent outside of his attacking arm and block with the back of the wrist sharply bent, forcing the attacking arm down in a rapid circular motion. This maneuver is made possible by the fact that the opponent's arm is already moving in a downward direction. Using the same hand, immediately attack the opponent's jaw with a palm-heel strike; then, pushing against his jaw, throw him over your knee and complete the counterattack with a punch to the face. For safety's sake, the hand holding the knife should be squeezed between the body and elbow during the throw.

D. When an opponent attempts an upward stabbing attack to the neck.
Dodge the blow by turning diagonally to the rear and leaning forward; then counterattack with a back thrust kick to the armpit.

E. When an opponent attempts a backhand slashing attack to the stomach.
Anticipating the attack, move in and block the attacking arm with a knife-hand block, forcing it down; quickly grasp the opponent's arm and counterattack with a reverse punch to the face.

F. When an opponent attempts an upward slashing attack.
With careful timing and distancing, lean back to dodge the attack and side snap kick to the armpit. To minimize the danger of a second attack, while kicking grasp the hand holding the knife.

G. When an opponent attempts a slashing attack to the legs.
Lift the leg as for an inside snapping block to dodge the attack; without lowering it to the ground, side thrust kick to the face. To prevent a second attack, grasp the opponent's arm while kicking.

H. When an opponent attempts a close slashing attack to the face or neck.
Fall sideward to dodge the attack; as the opponent brings his arm back in a backhand stab, counterattack with a back thrust kick to the ribs.

21
Defense against an Attack by a Club

The most important element in defending against attacks by such weapons is effective body shifting. After dodging outside of the attack, you must close in rapidly for the counterattack.

Examples of Defense against an Attack by a Club

A. When an opponent attempts a jabbing attack to the face with a club.

Block with an extended knife-hand block; then side thrust kick to the armpit (if the distance is too short, side snap kick). Lower the leg, grasp the opponent's attacking arm to throw him off balance, and reverse punch to his face.

B. When an opponent attempts a smashing attack to the top of the head with a club.

Anticipating the attack, push strongly against the elbow joint of the attacking arm; then slide in and counterattack with a forward elbow strike to the solar plexus.

C. When an opponent attempts a roundhouse attack to the temple with a club.

Block with a rising (knife-hand) block and simultaneously counterattack with a knife-hand strike to the neck. (See explanation of this technique on page 181.)

D. When an opponent attempts a back-hand attack to the face with a club.
With careful timing, lean sideways to dodge the attack, blocking with a sliding block and simultaneously counterattacking with a roundhouse kick to the face (or the solar plexus, or the groin).

E. When an opponent attempts a back-hand attack to the stomach with a club.
With careful timing, fall diagonally forward and counterattack with a roundhouse kick to the stomach.

F. When an opponent attempts a diagonal strike to the head or neck with a rod.

Quickly take one step back to dodge the blow. As the opponent brings his arm forward again in a back-hand strike, move in quickly and counterattack with a front kick to the armpit and a reverse punch to the face.

G. When an opponent threatens a back-hand strike to the stomach with a rod.

Dodge diagonally toward the opponent outside of the attack, leaning the body away from the direction of the attack and blocking with a sliding block; then counterattack with a roundhouse kick to the solar plexus.

H. When an opponent threatens a downward strike with a rod.

Dodge inside of the attack and block with an extended knife-hand block; then, throwing the opponent off balance, counterattack with a reverse punch to the face.

I. When an opponent threatens a downward strike with a pole

Move in with one step and block the pole with palms of both hands, the thumb side of the upper hand pointing downward and the thumb of the lower hand pointing forward. Move in farther with a sliding step, twist the pole and force it downward to throw the opponent off balance; then counterattack with a front kick to the solar plexus.

J. When an opponent threatens a back-hand strike to the legs with a pole.
Jump up to dodge the blow, simultaneously executing a front kick to the face; then complete the counterattack with a punch to the face.

K. When an opponent threatens a jabbing attack with a pole.
Dodge quickly to the inside of the attack, grasp the pole with both hands, assume a straddle-leg stance, and counterattack with a front kick to the solar plexus. For the sake of clarity, the last photograph was taken from the opposite side.

22
Defense against a Pistol Threat

When one is threatened by an assailant armed with a pistol from a distance, there's little that can be done other than bluff it out; or, if the opportunity presents itself, quickly seek cover. But in the event of a holdup at close range within reach of the hands or feet, karate techniques can be used to thwart the attack and to deliver an effective counterattack. One point to be especially borne in mind is the importance of finding and taking advantage of any lapses in the attacker's attention.

Examples of Defense against a Pistol Threat

A. When an opponent pushes a pistol against the stomach. Swing one hand quickly down to strike the hand holding the pistol with an open hand, forcing it away from your body; then, holding the opponent's hand firmly, counterattack with a front kick to the groin and a reverse punch to the face.

B. When an opponent a short distance to the front threatens with a pistol.

Side snap kick the arm holding the pistol; then quickly step in and counterattack with a reverse punch to the solar plexus. To avoid putting the opponent on his guard, the movements preparatory to kicking in this maneuver must be performed as subtly as possible.

C. When an opponent to the side holds a pistol against the temple.

Simultaneously turn the body and ward off the pistol with a knife-hand block; then, holding the opponent's hand, counterattack with a knife-hand strike to the neck.

D. When an opponent a short distance to the side threatens with a pistol.

In one movement, twist the body, block downward with a knife-hand block, and counterattack with a roundhouse kick to the chest.

E. When an opponent presses a pistol into the small of the back.

Simultaneously turn, step back, and block with a downward block; then grasp the opponent's pistol hand, pull him off balance, and counterattack with a forward elbow strike to the solar plexus.

Appendix:
Karate Equipment and Its Use

Punching Board

The punching board (*makiwara*) is a piece of equipment unique to karate and is especially essential in toughening the hands and giving training in hand techniques. It consists merely of a straight board with a portion at the top fitted for punching. The board itself is made from a four-by-four that is 7 or 8 feet long. The top

4 feet are beveled down so that the very top is about ½ inch thick. In Japan, the striking surface of the punching board has traditionally consisted of a bundle of straw with a ½-inch straw rope tightly wound around it at the top part of the board for about a foot. Recently, a piece of sponge rubber 2 inches thick, 4 inches wide, and 12 inches long, covered with canvas, has come into wide use.

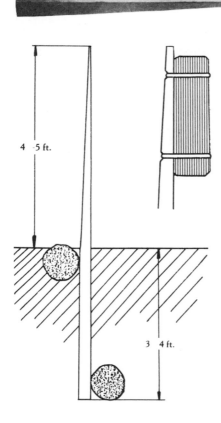

How to make and install

1. Dig a hole in the ground 3 or 4 feet deep. Plant the unbeveled end of the board in it so that the top reaches a point near the top of the chest, and pack with small and large stones, as shown in the diagram. Concrete will serve the purpose even better. After planting, the top of the board should move 5 or 6 inches without exerting too much pressure. It is better to have the board too flexible than not flexible enough.

2. Attach the straw and straw rope or canvas-covered sponge (with strong, fine twine) near the top of the board so that the center of the striking surface comes to a height even with the solar plexus.

Purpose

- A punching board is an excellent way to get the feel of karate techniques applied to an actual target, rather than into the empty air. It gives practice in focusing, muscular control, breath control, etc.
- Use of the punching board develops stronger techniques.
- It is a convenient way to toughen the skin of the knuckles and other striking points. Because it is difficult to master the technique of focus, i.e., concentration of strength at the moment of impact, without practicing on a punching board, many karate experts feel that the techniques of those who don't use one are bound to lack power.

How to use

The punching board is used mainly for practicing hand techniques, although foot techniques also are sometimes practiced on it. Shown here are some typical examples of its use with hand techniques. In all cases, the point of focus is about two inches on the other side of the board when it is stationary. At the point of impact, sharply let out a short breath, breathing in while withdrawing. This gives good training in breath control.

A. Reverse punch

This is one of the most basic techniques of karate and must be practiced constantly by beginners as well as experts. Unlike the striking techniques, which almost invariably depend on the use of a snapping motion, focusing the punch is not easy to learn merely by practicing it into the empty air. In preparing to punch the board, stand directly in front of it in a forward stance at such a distance that the fist extends about two inches beyond the board when the arm is fully extended. In punching, rotate the hips fully back, but without shifting balance, and extend the opposite hand forward; then perform the reverse punch at the board. Take care to strike correctly with the four
striking points of the fore-fist. There will be a tendency for the hand to glance off at first, but constant practice will correct this. In punching, if anything the hips should be lowered toward the target, rather than raised. About one hundred punches with each hand is reasonable for one practice session.

B. Back-fist strike

Stand in a straddle-leg stance at a 45° angle to the board. Execute a sideward strike to the board, fully utilizing the snap of the elbow. A variation which makes the blow more effective is to start from a forward stance and then to twist into a straddle-leg stance while striking.

C. Knife-hand strike

Assume a forward stance to the side of the board. To execute either an inside or outside strike, twist the hips back and then forward. To avoid injury be sure to hold fingers firmly together.

D. Ridge-hand strike

Follow the same stance and procedure as above to execute an outside strike.

E. Elbow strike

Follow the same stance and procedure as for a reverse punch, but closer to the board, to practice a forward strike.

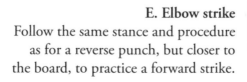

Punching and Kicking Bag

There are two sizes of punching bags commonly used in karate, one 3½ feet long and 1½ feet thick, and the other 1 foot long and 6 inches thick. Both consist of leather or rubber waste stuffed tightly into a canvas bag. They should be hung so that the bottom comes about even with the groin. The longer one is best hung by a rope or chain that will enable it to be conveniently raised and lowered. The smaller bag should be hung on a strong rubber band, such as a bicycle tube.

Purpose
- The large bag is used mainly for practicing focusing and for strengthening the various kicks. It gives excellent training in perfecting the most effective angle of impact.
- The smaller bag is also used for kicking practice. Since it is light and is hung on an elastic band, it will move when struck, giving good practice in timing and in kicking a moving target.
- Both bags can also be used for practicing hand techniques, and particularly hand and foot techniques in combination.

Punching Ball

This consists of a rubber ball about 1 foot in diameter placed inside a leather bag fastened to the ceiling and floor with strong rubber ropes. The center of the ball should be about shoulder height.

Purpose

The punching ball is used mainly for practice in the timing of hand techniques. It is also useful for kicking practice.

Body Stretcher

Pieces of equipment similar to this and with the same purpose are found in many other sports and will serve as well as the one shown here. The main purpose is to toughen the muscles of the stomach, abdomen, and sides. The stretcher shown here is constructed in such a way that the horizontal board can be adjusted to fit the length of the legs of the person using it.

(See explanation of use on page 46.)

Dumbbells

For karate training, dumbbells weighing from 3 to 5 pounds are best. They are effective in strengthening the muscles used in extending and retracting the arms.

Be sure to keep the shoulders down and to tense the chest muscles adequately. If this is not done, focusing of hand techniques will be hindered rather than helped. Since the use of dumbbells sacrifices speed for strength, after using them it is a good idea to practice a bit without them.

Iron Geta (*clogs*)

This is a piece of equipment unique to karate. They weigh about 5 pounds each, their use doing for the legs what the dumbbells do for the arms. After using them, it is desirable to perform a few kicks without them.

Heavy Club

This is either a heavy wooden club or an iron pipe weighing about 10 pounds. It should be 5 to 6 feet long and have a handle fixed for easy holding. It gives good training in balance and focusing and provides general muscle-strengthening exercise.

How to use

As shown here, swing the club over your head and stop it smartly in front of your body; or swing it from the side and stop it smartly in front of your body.

Pulleys

Attach two pulleys to the ceiling about 5 feet apart and pass a thin, strong rope through them so that both ends reach the floor. Fix the ends so they can be conveniently attached to the feet. These are useful for limbering-up and stretching the leg muscles. They can also be used to help train the leg muscles to kick properly.

How to use
Attach one foot to one end of the rope and pull the other end with both hands, stretching the leg up either forward or sideward. Also, as shown below, pull the rope with one hand to practice correct kicking form.

Mirror

A full-length mirror will be extremely useful in observing and correcting your form while practicing the various techniques.

Glossary

age-zuki	rising punch	*kake-waza*	hooking (techniques)
age-uke	rising block	*kakiwake-uke*	wedge block
choku-zuki	straight punch	*kakutō*	bent wrist
ch'uan fa	"fist way"	*kakutō-uke*	bent-wrist block
dōjō	(training) gym	*kata*	"forms"
empi	elbow	*keitō*	chicken-head wrist
empi-uchi	elbow strike	*keitō-uke*	chicken-head-wrist block
fumikomi	stamping kick	*kempō*	"fist way"
fumi-waza	stamping (techniques)	*kendō*	sword fighting
gedan-barai	downward block	*keri-waza*	kicking (techniques)
geta	clogs	*kiba-dachi*	straddle-leg stance
gyaku-zuki	reverse punch	*kihon kumite*	basic sparring
hachiji-dachi	open-leg stance	*kime*	focus
hangetsu-dachi	wide hourglass stance	*kokō*	tiger-mouth hand
haishu	back hand	*kōkutsu-dachi*	back stance
haishu-uchi	back-hand strike	*koshi*	ball of the foot
haishu-uke	back-hand block	*kumade*	bear hand
haisoku	instep	*kumite*	sparring
haitō	ridge hand	*ma-ai*	distancing
haitō-uchi	ridge-hand strike	*mae-geri*	front kick
heisoku-dachi	informal-attention stance	*mae-geri-keage*	front snap kick
hen-ō	responding	*mae-geri-kekomi*	front thrust kick
hiraken	fore-knuckle fist	*mae-tobi-geri*	flying front kick
hiraken-zuki	fore-knuckle-fist straight punch	*makiwara*	punching board
hittsui	knee	*mawashi-geri*	roundhouse kick
hittsui-geri	knee kick	*mawashi-zuki*	roundhouse punch
ippon-ken	one-knuckle fist	*mikazuki-geri*	crescent kick
ippon-ken-zuki	one-knuckle-fist straight punch	*mikazuki-geri-uke*	crescent-kick block
ippon-nukite	one-finger spear hand	*mizu no kokoro*	"mind like water"
jiyū-ippon-kumite	semi-free one-blow sparring	*morote-uke*	augmented forearm block
jiyu-kumite	freestyle sparring	*morote-zuki*	double-fist punch
jūji-uke	X-block	*nagashi-uke*	sweeping block
kagi-zuki	hook punch	*nage-waza*	throwing (techniques)
kakato	heel	*nakadate-ippon-ken*	middle-finger one-knuckle fist
kake-dameshi	tests of strength	*nami-ashi*	inside snapping block
kake-uke	hooking block	*neko-ashi-dachi*	cat stance

nihon-nukite	two-finger spear hand	*teisoku*	sole
nukite	spear-hand straight thrust	*tettsui*	bottom fist
oi-zuki	lunge punch	*tettsui-uchi*	bottom-fist strike
Okinawa-te	"Okinawa hands"	*tettsui-uke*	bottom-fist block
osae-uke	pressing block	*tsukami-uke*	grasping block
riken	back fist	*tsuki no kokoro*	"mind like the moon"
riken-uchi	back-fist strike	*tsuki-uke*	punching block
sanchin-dachi	hourglass stance	*tsuki-waza*	punching (techniques)
seiken	fore-fist	*uchi-waza*	striking (techniques)
seiken-choku-zuki	fore-fist straight punch	*ude*	forearm
seiryūtō	ox-jaw hand	*ude-uke*	forearm block
shutō	knife hand	*ura-zuki*	close punch
shutō-uchi	knife-hand strike	*ushiro-geri*	back kick
shutō-uke	knife-hand block	*ushiro-geri-keage*	back snap kick
sōchin-dachi	diagonal straddle-leg stance	*ushiro-geri-kekomi*	back thrust kick
sokutō	foot edge	*yama-zuki*	U-punch
suki	opening	*yoko-geri*	side kick
sukui-uke	scooping block	*yoko-geri-keage*	side snap kick
tate-zuki	vertical-fist punch	*yoko-geri-kekomi*	side thrust kick
teishō	palm heel	*yoko-tobi-geri*	flying side kick
teishō-uchi	palm-heel strike	*yonhon-nukite*	spear hand
teishō-uke	palm-heel block	*zenkutsu-dachi*	forward stance
teishō-zuki	palm-heel straight punch		

Index

ABOUT TUTTLE
"Books to Span the East and West"

Our core mission at Tuttle Publishing is to create books which bring people together one page at a time. Tuttle was founded in 1832 in the small New England town of Rutland, Vermont (USA). Our fundamental values remain as strong today as they were then—to publish best-in-class books informing the English-speaking world about the countries and peoples of Asia. The world has become a smaller place today and Asia's economic, cultural and political influence has expanded, yet the need for meaningful dialogue and information about this diverse region has never been greater. Since 1948, Tuttle has been a leader in publishing books on the cultures, arts, cuisines, languages and literatures of Asia. Our authors and photographers have won numerous awards and Tuttle has published thousands of books on subjects ranging from martial arts to paper crafts. We welcome you to explore the wealth of information available on Asia at www.tuttlepublishing.com.

Published by Tuttle Publishing, an imprint of Periplus Editions (HK) Ltd.

www.tuttlepublishing.com

Copyright © 2019 by Charles E. Tuttle Publishing Co., Inc.

Library of Congress Cataloging-in-Publication Data

LCC Card No. 59010409

ISBN 978-0-8048-5122-0

First edition
22 21 20 19   6 5 4 3 2   1904CM
Printed in China

DISTRIBUTED BY

North America, Latin America & Europe
Tuttle Publishing
364 Innovation Drive
North Clarendon, VT 05759-9436 U.S.A.
Tel: (802) 773-8930
Fax: (802) 773-6993
info@tuttlepublishing.com
www.tuttlepublishing.com

Japan
Tuttle Publishing
Yaekari Building, 3rd Floor
5-4-12 Osaki, Shinagawa-ku
Tokyo 141 0032
Tel: (81) 3 5437-0171
Fax: (81) 3 5437-0755
sales@tuttle.co.jp
www.tuttle.co.jp

Asia Pacific
Berkeley Books Pte. Ltd.
3 Kallang Sector, #04-01
Singapore 349278
Tel: (65) 6741 2178
Fax: (65) 6741 2179
inquiries@periplus.com.sg
www.periplus.com